CW00350291

THE CHANGING

Kennington

BOOK ONE

Carole Newbigging

Robert Boyd
PUBLICATIONS

Published by
Robert Boyd Publications
260 Colwell Drive
Witney, Oxfordshire OX8 7LW

First published 1999

Copyright © Carole Newbigging and
Robert Boyd Publications

ISBN: 1 899536 43 4

All rights reserved. No part of this book may be produced, stored in a retrieval system, or transmitted, in any form or by any means, electronic, mechanical, photocopying, recording or otherwise, without the prior approval of the publisher.

TITLES IN THE *CHANGING FACES* SERIES

Banbury: Book One
The Bartons
Bicester: Book One *and* Book Two
Bladon with Church Hanborough and
    Long Hanborough
Botley and North Hinksey: Book One
    and Book Two
Chipping Norton: Book One
St Clements and East Oxford:
    Book One *and* Book Two
Cowley: Book One, Book Two *and*
    Book Three
Cowley Works: Book One
Cumnor and Farmoor with Appleton
    and Eaton
St Ebbes and St Thomas: Book One
    and Book Two
Eynsham: Book One *and* Book Two
Faringdon and District
Grimsbury
Headington: Book One *and* Book Two
Iffley
Jericho: Book One *and* Book Two
Kennington
Littlemore and Sandford

Marston: Book One *and* Book Two
North Oxford: Book One *and* Book Two
Oxford City Centre: Book One
South Oxford: Book One *and* Book Two
Summertown and Cutteslowe
West Oxford
Witney: Book One
Wolvercote with Wytham and Godstow
Woodstock: Book One *and* Book Two
Yarnton with Cassington and Begbroke

FORTHCOMING

Abingdon
Banbury: Book Two
Blackbird Leys
Charlbury
Cowley Works: Book Two
Easington
Florence Park
Grimsbury: Book Two
Littlemore and Sandford: Book Two
Oxford City Centre: Book Two
Rose Hill
Thame
Witney: Book Two

Printed and bound in Great Britain at The Alden Press, Oxford

Contents

Front cover photograph

The Tandem pre 1920, with 'Hooky' Walker and Mrs Walker, landlords.

Back cover photograph

The Chasney family c1939 in the grounds of The Tandem. Horace Chasney is on the left, Joan Perks the family 'help' on the horse held by Eric Chasney, Betty Chasney riding Flower Show, the pedigree Guernsey held by Ray Chasney, June Chasney on the donkey with mother Lilian and Norman Chasney.

Dedication

This book is dedicated to Ray Chasney, landlord of The Tandem from June 1958 to October 1982, in recognition of his unique knowledge of Kennington and its people.

Acknowledgements

Kennington is fortunate in having an excellent collection of material, through the efforts of the Kennington History Project. It is with grateful thanks that I acknowledge this collection, from which I have gleaned the majority of factual information within this book. In particular, I am grateful to Shirley Jones for permission to consult the material within the collection, to Peter Baker and Peter Hooper, to Stanley Gillam for kind permission to quote and extract from his work *The Story of Kennington*, and to Mrs Winifred Spray for permission to use extracts from her work *The Kennington Memorial Field*. The collection of personal memoirs provided excellent background material from which I have extracted some of the quotations contained in this book, in particular the memoirs of Alan and Gwen Green, Charlie Kerby, Len Peedell, Cyril Peedell, Hettie Perkins, Maurice Petts, Reg and Lily Taylor, Gladys Theobald, and Ted Wichall.

In addition I thank the following residents, past and present, who have given freely of their time, helped to identify names, and kindly allowed me to use their own photographs and material: Joan Benwell, Margaret Biggs, Mrs Doreen Box, Ray Chasney, Doreen Cox, David Eggleton, Barry and Yvonne Enock, Jack and Doris Francis, Ron Harris, Pam Hill, Mr and Mrs Ken Johnson, Idris Jones, Audrey Kerby, Mrs Joy Ledger, Arthur and Eileen Marshall, Pat O'Reilly, Wendy Patrick, Maureen Pope, June Poole, Pauline Roberts, George and Carol Ross, Gerald Shayler, Ray and Margaret Simpson, Tony and Rose Taylor, Gwyneth Thomas, Mandy Taylor, Sylvia Rivers, Dennis and Kathleen Tasker, George and Betty Trinder, Les Wacknell, Muriel Woodruff and Gladys Wyatt.

It is hoped this book will give an insight into Kennington's history, while recording some of the events that have gone into making that history. A second book is planned and further material would be welcome.

Finally, I would apologise to anyone whom I have inadvertently omitted to thank, and for any incorrect names that may appear here in print. I would ask readers to remember that all names, facts and dates are subject to the frailty of human memory and while every effort is made for accuracy, errors do, inevitably, creep in.

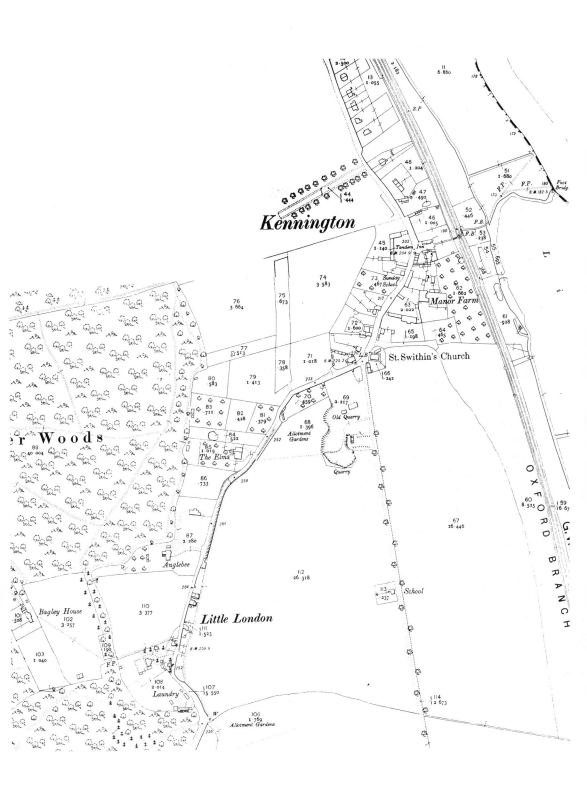

Kennington Map 1913

Who was St Swithun?

St Swithun's Day, if thou dost rain,
For forty days it will remain;
St Swithun's Day, if thou be fair,
For forty days 'twill rain nae mair.

Swithun, also spelled Swithin, was born in Wessex, England and was educated at Winchester, where he was ordained. He became chaplain to King Egberg of the West Saxons, who appointed him tutor of his son, Ethelwulf, and was one of the King's counsellors. Swithun was made Bishop of Winchester in A.D. 852 when Ethelwulf succeeded his father as King. Swithun built several churches and was known for his humility and aid to the poor and needy.

A well known superstition states that should it rain on his feast day, 15th July, then it will rain for forty days. The origin of this belief is unknown, but the following was reported in the press some years ago:

Bishop Swithun (or Swithin) of Winchester died in A.D. 862 with a prayer that he be buried not within the church but outside in 'a vile and unworthy place, under the drip of eaves, where the rain of heaven might fall upon him.'. He was duly buried, according to the chroniclers Lanfrid and Wolstan, between the north wall and wooden belfry tower.

During the following century there were several miracles attributed to St Swithun, by praying at his tomb. Consequently, on 15 July 971, the remains of Swithun was moved from his original resting place inside the new church of St Peter's minster. More miracles occurred; two hundred sufferers were said to have been healed within ten days. Swithun was also reported to have made several appearances, on one occasion rebuking the local monks. A few years later he was adopted as this church's patron saint, remaining so until the time of Henry VIII.

Apparently the weather had been fine and sunny during the time of the translation of St Swithun's body; why then the connection with rain? According to Brand in Popular Antiquities, Swithun was apparently furious at being moved inside the church. Heavy rain began to fall during the operation and continued for forty days as 'a warning from heaven to let him lie in peace and respect his dying wish.'

St Swithun's Church

The church of St Swithun's, Kennington in 1930. The two cottages on the right hand side were demolished in 1936 when the ground on which the vicarage and the new church now stand was acquired.

In Norman times there was mention of a chapel at Kennington dedicated to St Swithun, who was Saxon Bishop of Winchester between 838 and 862. The dedication of the church to a Saxon saint indicates its early origin, because such dedications found disfavour after the Norman Conquest.

Until 1866 Kennington was not an ecclesiastical parish. The chapel was a chapel-of-ease to neighbouring Sunningwell and the services were normally conducted by a curate from that parish, which included part of Kennington, the remainder being in the parish of Radley. By 1783 the old chapel building was no longer in existence. At that time Joseph Bennet, Rector of Sunningwell, stated that *'there was a Chapel of Ease within a mile and a half or two miles of Sunningwell; there are now no remains of it.'* The church was rebuilt in 1828 on the same foundations by Rev Henry Bowyer, the Rector of Sunningwell. The unofficial Bowyer crest of an archer (a bowyer) may be seen on the capital of the right hand pillar of the doorway. The capital on the left is carved with their official crest of a falcon rising.

Incumbents of St Swithun's Church, Kennington

1829-54	Peter Maurice	Curate
1854-56	Frederick George Lee	Curate
1856-59	Thomas Julius Henderson	Curate
1860-62	William George Longden	Curate
1862-65	Compton Reade	Curate
1865-68	Samuel Lilckendey Warren	Vicar
1868-73	John Henry Blunt	Vicar
1874-75	William M Bebb	Vicar
1876-1903	George Charles Bliss	Vicar
1904-18	Charles Boxall Longland	Vicar
1905-14	Richard Morgan Rees	Curate
1918-37	Charles Abdy Marcon	Vicar
1929-37	John Charles Trevelyan	Curate
1937-46	Thomas Hearne Liddiard	Vicar
1946-52	John Henry Sladen Dixon	Vicar
1952-65	Stuart Simeon Davies	Vicar
1965-79	Harold A T Bennett	Vicar
1979-84	John Michael Loveland	Vicar
1984-98	Harry Bloomfield	Vicar

Charles Longland was vicar of Radley from 1898 until 1916 and also of Kennington from 1904 until 1918, during which time the ecclesiastical parishes of Radley and Kennington were officially united.

The Rev Marcon died in 1953, aged ninety-nine, and in 1956 his daughter donated a pair of Sheffield plate candlesticks to the church in memory of her parents. From 1929 until his retirement in 1937, Marcon was assisted by an elderly cleric, John Charles Trevelyan, who lived at St Veep's House, Bagley Wood Road, with his sister, Miss Trevelyan, a school governor.

Looking north along Kennington Lane. This view is taken from a postcard dated 13 June 1930. Note the iron railings in front of the church.

The Vicarage

By the 1850s a cottage, which stood on a site to the north of the Tandem, was made available in the village as a residence for the vicar. This was, perhaps, the cottage and grounds purchased by Sir George Bowyer, 3rd baronet, from Martha Roberts in 1839. Sir George's uncle, Henry Bowyer, was Rector of Sunningwell from 1812 until his death in 1853, and, as such, would have had an interest in the housing of the Curates. This property was known as The Parsonage. In 1873 William Bebb, third vicar of Kennington, asked for a site for a permanent vicarage. However, more than sixty years passed before Kennington's vicars were provided with a purpose-built home.

In 1935 John Trevelyan paid £350 to Mrs Emily Copp, the widow of John Copp, former owner of the Manor Farm, for the land on which the vicarage and new church now stand. He paid another £300 on demolishing the cottages which stood upon the land, building a boundary wall and providing a gateway. The land intended as the site of the vicarage was conveyed to the Ecclesiastical Commissioners, who estimated the cost of building in the region of £2,000. Building started on 1st November 1937. John Trevelyan died before the end of the war.

Proposed
alterations 1914.

In 1867 the vicar was asked to find out the legal costs for the transfer and consecration of a piece of land behind the church for use as a burial ground. This land belonged to Sir George Bowyer and was let to Job Mundy of the Manor Farm. However, this idea did not come to fruition, and, by a deed dated 22 January 1913, Edgar Norton Disney gave two pieces of land to the church, one of which was the present burial ground in Sandford Lane. This area of land, part of the Manor Farm, was known as Sour Close.

The other gift of land in 1913, some 222 square yards immediately behind the church, was proposed for an extension to the church. A committee was set up, comprising the vicar, the Rev Longland, Dr W Tyrrell Brooks of Bagley Wood and P H King of 'The Hawthorns' Kennington. The extension would have provided seats for two hundred people, at an estimated cost of £1,200. The site is now the present church hall.

Gwen Fensome seen here in the early 1940s, standing in the fields where the new church is now situated.

The Rev Stuart Davies was appointed vicar in 1952 and wasted no time in pressing ahead with the idea of building a new church. Seen here c1954, with Mrs M Pearson, Mrs L Nash and Miss F M Blunson, he sat outside for twelve hours to receive £85 in gifts to help pay for the building of the new church. Of the £20,000 required there was still £4,700 outstanding.

Other contributions being collected, left to right: Gillian Boult, Irene Morris, −, Rev Stuart Davies, Gillian Dugmore, Yvonne Wyatt, Margaret Francis. Mrs MacDonald and Jeannette MacDonald are behind the wall.

Church choir in 1957, left to right back row: Edward Keep, Chris Spragg, Barry Perkins, Richard Simms, Rev Stuart Davies, Geoffrey Nash, Mr Bert Horseman, John Francis, John Simms, Mark Horseman. Front row: Brian Goldsworthy, Brian Jones, John Grant, Andrew Chalmers.

The new church of St Swithun's, 1999

On 6 July 1956 the Oxford Mail reported: '... *ending on Sunday 15 July, the Feast of St Swithun, Kennington celebrates the thousandth anniversary of the village, which is being honoured by the beginning of a permanent memorial, a new church.'*

Built in the grounds of the old church, adjacent to the vicarage, the foundation stone was laid on Saturday 15 September 1956 by Dr H J Carpenter, Bishop of Oxford. The design by the architect, T Lawrence Dale, was modern, with a central altar, from ideas put forward by the Rev Stuart Davies. Building costs of £13,000 were accepted at a meeting of the parish council on 23 July 1956 and a week later the site was consecrated by the Bishop of Reading.

In 1965 a statue of Our Lady and Child was placed in the niche on the righthand side of the Church, following the wishes of the late Ernest James Blackwell, who left a legacy with the request that this should be done in memory of his brother. The two-manual organ was acquired in 1982 in memory of Bert Horseman, organist for 23 years.

SECTION TWO

The Manor House and Farm

The first mention of Kennington would appear to be in the year 956, in the Chronicles of Abingdon Abbey. In that year King Edwig of Wessex made a charter granting Kennington to a priest called Byrhtelm, who later conferred it to the Abbot of Abingdon in exchange for Curbridge in Oxfordshire. There have been various spellings of Kennington, including Cenigtun and Kenitune meaning Kenings town, or the settlement of Cena's people. The Anglo Saxon word Cene means bold, valiant and keen.

The land remained in the possession of Abingdon Abbey until the dissolution in 1538 when it was divided between two families, the Crokes and the Lyons. John Croke owned land in Kennington in 1538 and John Lyon, an alderman of London, was granted land at Kennington together with the manor of Northcourt in Abingdon.

In 1802, at the time of the Inclosure, Kennington was a small village in the centre of extensive farm land, together with a hamlet, Little London, along the present Bagley Wood Road. At this time the population was less than 100, all employed in agriculture. The Kennington Road, then known as Oxford Road, led only to the village, although Abingdon could be accessed via Bagley Wood Road, then called Abingdon Road. There were several footpaths throughout the area, namely Little London Path; Radley Foot Path entered from Cow Lane and following the line of the present day Avenue; Iffley Ferry Path alongside The Fish public house, now the Tandem; and Bagley Wood Path, which is possibly the existing path from Kennington Road leading to Rowles Close and Upper Road.

The Inclosure Act of 1802 resulted in Sir George Bowyer of Radley (1783-1860) being allotted some land in the township, and, following extensive land purchases, he eventually became Lord of the Manor. Following his death in 1860 a valuation of the Kennington Estate was carried out by James Saunders of Oxford for Sir George Bowyer, the new baronet. The size of the Estate is given as 477 acres, of which 387 acres were held by Stephen Mundy, tenant of Manor Farm.

Sir George Bowyer, 3rd baronet, died in 1883, at which time the Kennington Estate was mortgaged to Colonel Edgar John Disney of Ingatestone, Essex. He foreclosed on the mortgage and this transfer was confirmed in 1887. Colonel Disney died in 1903 and the Estate was taken over by his son, Edgar Norton Disney.

The Manor Farmhouse seen from Kennington Road 1913. (J A L Myers)

The Manor House is believed to have been built in 1629 by Oliver Smith and Henry Bosworth, rich brewers of Oxford, following the marriage, in 1627, of their children, John, Oliver's third son, and Elizabeth, Henry's daughter. There is a date of 1629 carved on a corbel in a ground floor room, together with the initials OS and HB. By 1660 the property had become part of a farm — known as Smiths Farm — the whole of which was let. John Smith died in 1657, and his son, also John, in 1671. The property passed to the family of a married sister, and was thus owned by Henry Turner in 1716. During this period it was occupied by various tenants, including John Pead, John and Margaret Greenaway, and Mr Danby and John Pilliard.

The rear of Manor Farmhouse in 1913. (J A L Myers)

The Manor Farm, as part of Kennington Estate, was purchased in 1809 by Sir George Bowyer, 2nd baronet, but subsequently mortgaged to Thomas Hamlet, a goldsmith of Leicester, from whom it was purchased in 1846 by the Rev Henry Bowyer. The farm house itself was described as *'formerly in the occupation of John Pilliard, John Greenaway, John Tubb, John Bannister and late of John Gee.'* It is not known when the title Manor Farm first came into use, but the Mundy family were tenants from shortly after the purchase by Sir George Bowyer for at least 90 years, probably longer. Stephen Mundy senior was born about 1761, living at Kennington in 1841 with a male and two female servants. His son, also Stephen, born 1789, took over the Manor Farm in 1823. At the time of his death, 2 December 1860, the farm buildings were *'very dilapidated'* but the Farm House was described as being in good repair. Stephen's widow, Maria, remained but by 1871 the youngest son, Job, then aged 31, was in charge. The farm was the main occupation in Kennington, and the Mundy family employed men by the names of Godfrey, Greenaway, Poole, Steptoe, Wheeler, Silvester, Champ, Earles and Darling, all long established Kennington family names.

Job Mundy died about 1906 and his widow Elizabeth carried on, but the Mundy family connection ended in 1913 when the Kennington Estate was sold. Lot 15 of this sale was the Manor Farm and four cottages, in size totalling 250 acres of thereabouts, at a rent of £237 16s.

The Manor Farmhouse viewed from the garden in 1913. (J A L Myers)

The sale catalogue of Kennington Estate in 1913 describes the Farm House and states that at that time the front door was between the two windows to the north of the building. In September 1917 the Manor Farm House came on the market again. It had been updated, and the front door moved to its present position. It was stated as including a bathroom *'with hot and cold supplies and WC'*, with water, of good quality, being supplied by a force pump.

The property was purchased in 1938 by the late Dr J N L Myres of Christ Church, in whose family it still remains.

SUMMARY OF LOTS.

Lot	Property.	Tenant.	Acreage.			Rent or Rental Value.		
			A.	R.	P.	£	s.	d.
1	Building Site	In Hand	0	1	23			
2	Do.	Do.	0	2	39			
3	Do.	Do.	0	1	7			
4	Do.	Do.	0	1	4			
5	Do.	Do.	0	1	2			
6	Do.	Do.	0	1	2			
7	Do.	Do.	0	1	2	8	10	0
8	Do.	Do.	0	1	2			
9	Do.	Do.	0	1	1			
10	Do.	Do.	0	1	1			
11	Do.	Do.	0	1	1			
12	Do.	Do.	0	1	1			
13	Do.	Do.	0	1	1			
14	Do.	Do.	0	1	1			
15	Kennington Manor Farm, etc.	Mrs. Mundy and others ...	250	0	36	275	9	0
16	Small Holding (Arable) ...	Mrs. Mundy	5	2	4	5	15	0
17	Do. (Pasture) ...	Do.	1	1	31	3	10	0
18	Do. (do.) ...	Mrs. Mundy & Mr. Walker	0	2	33	1	15	0
19	Yard and Buildings ...	Mrs. Mundy	0	3	36	6	10	0
20	Orchard	Do.	0	2	15	2	0	0
21	Three Cottages, etc. ...	Various	0	1	37	13	0	0
22	Do. ...	Do.	0	2	1	16	8	0
23	Two Cottages, etc.	Messrs. Gibbons & Villabois	0	1	23	15	12	0
24	Cottage and Garden ...	Mr. T. Allen	0	0	31	15	0	0
25	Small Holding, etc. ...	Mr. East and Various ...	1	0	23	13	5	0
26	Building Site	Mrs. Mundy and Various	1	2	10	1	19	4
27	Do.	Mrs. Mundy	1	3	7	1	10	0
28	Do.	Do.	1	1	37	1	10	0
29	Do.	Miss Slay	0	0	16	1	0	0
30	Meadow—Fidlers Elbow ...	In Hand	6	1	33	7	0	0
31	Freehold Ground Rent ...	Mrs. Basson	0	0	20	2	0	0
32	Do. ...	Mr. J. P. Weller... ...	0	0	20	2	0	0
33	Do. ...	Messrs. Herbert & Boulton	0	0	31	4	0	0
34	Do. ...	Mr. A. J. Faulkner ...	0	0	38	4	0	0
35	Do. ...	Mr. Wm. Faulkner ...	0	0	38	4	0	0
36	Do. ...	Mr. C. E. T. Richmond...	1	0	0	5	0	0
37	Do. ...	Mr. E. E. J. English ...	0	3	27	5	5	0
38	Do. ...	Miss Slay...	1	2	22	10	10	0
		Totals	A.282	1	16	£426	8	4

Summary of Lots — from the 1913 Sale Catalogue.

Although some land was sold by the Disney family in 1911, the 13th May 1913 may be regarded as the birthday of modern Kennington. At this time the Estate was divided into 38 Lots for auction.

The Barn and Byre, originally part of Manor Farm.

The Kennington Estate of 1913 amounted to some 282 acres, 250 of which comprised the Manor Farm with its barns, sheds and outbuildings. The farm itself was Lot 15, and included the cottage now known as The Onion Patch and properties to the south of the Manor House, being the former blacksmith's shop. It also included Winter's Orchard, the site of Otter's Reach. Lot 15 was sold to a James Bradfield for £5,530, and was sold by him in 1918 to John Copp.

Looking north towards the Tandem c1910, with the corner of Cow Lane on the right hand side. Wych-Elm Cottage, now known as The Onion Patch, is on the right. Jasmine Cottage is on the left in the middle distance, with the magnificent walnut tree opposite. The lady walking towards the Tandem, with a beer jug in her hand, is Mrs Annie Giles.

Jasmine Cottage on the right hand side of this group of three cottages, seen here c1950 looking north. Lot 21 of the 1913 sale comprised three cottages, estate numbers 66, 67 and 68. Number 66 was let to R Gibbons, number 67 to Mrs Greenaway and number 68 to Mrs Steptoe. These cottages, sold for £145, were those at 206, 208 and 210 Kennington Road.

Jasmine Cottage, number 208, looking south. Note the door which was later converted to a window. *'Jinny Steptoe lived in the cottage opposite the Barn and Byre. She used to spend a lot of the time just sitting by her door. Behind the wall on the other side of the road there was a huge walnut tree belonging to the Manor House and the children used to come along when the walnuts were ripe and Jinny would always shout 'Now you boys you leave that alone. I'm in charge of that tree and the walnuts'. She was a proper old lady: short and rather fat with grey hair and long black shirts. She seemed ever so old at the time. Her cottage was very small; two cottages are now made into one, and she lived in the cottage later occupied by Olive Horton, number 208.'*

The group of cottages on the right hand side stood opposite Cow Lane, and comprised Lot 22 of the 1913 sale catalogue. In the centre can be seen the rick-yard that stood opposite the present-day site of the war memorial.

A very early drawing, believed to date from 1815, of the same cottages viewed from the south.

The remains of these same cottages can be seen on the left hand side. The house now on this site was occupied by Dr Blackman for many years, and used as a surgery. The remains of a cottage fire grate can still be seen in a side wall in the front garden.

Woodbine Cottage, 2 Little London, was purchased by Sir George Bowyer in 1856 for the sum of £325. The property was Lot 24 in the 1913 sale, at which time it was let to Thomas Allen for £15 a year plus rates, who later purchased it freehold. It was brick built and tiled, containing two sitting rooms, kitchen, dairy and wash-house, three bedrooms and box room and a good garden. This building was the original village shop and bakery.

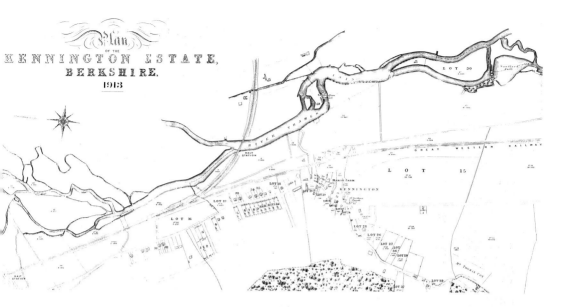

Of the remaining lots in the 1913 sale Lot 2 was the largest and was sold for £60. This was a half-acre building site on the north corner of Kenville Road and Upper Road, with frontages of 290ft and 108ft respectively. Lot 3, just over a quarter of an acre on the north corner of Kenville Road and Kennington Road, was sold to a Mr J P Weller for £30, and was eventually developed about 1930.

Lot 17 was pasture let to Mrs Munday and is now the site of 107 to 123 Kennington Road; Lot 18 was a smallholding directly opposite Edward Road with a frontage to Kennington Road of about 82 feet, extending back to the railway. This was purchased, probably by Alfred Faulkner a builder in Kennington. It became the site of the old memorial hall, now numbers 161 and 163 Kennington Road.

Lot 33 is now numbers 131 and 133 Kennington Road; Lots 34 and 35 are now 145 to 151 Kennington Road; part of Lot 19 was a farm house, buildings and yard, now the site of the Village Hall and Social Club; Lot 20, known as 'The Orchard', was the site of the old Sunday School and the present day medical centre and Lot 30, known as Fiddlers Elbow, an area of meadowland near the island towards Sandford, fetched £105.

From Kennington Chronicle 1950, provided by Abingdon Rural District Council			
	North	South	Total
Number of Houses	269	254	523
Rateable Value	4597	6530★	
Number of Electors	605	566	1171
Population (est.)	941	889	1830★★
Area acres est.	992	377	

★ includes cold storage depot, rateable value £1,700
★★ population of Ecclesiastical Parish must be some 60 less as it does not include parts of Sandford Lane.

KENNINGTON is a small village, and was formed into an ecclesiastical parish February 16th, 1866, out of the parishes of Radley and Sunningwell; it is separated from Oxfordshire by the river Isis and is on the high road from Oxford to Abingdon, 2 miles south from the former, 4 north from Abingdon and 2 miles north from Radley station on the Birmingham and Oxford branch of the Great Western railway, in the Northern division of the county, hundred of Hormer, petty sessional division, union and county court district of Abingdon, and in the rural deanery of Abingdon, archdeaconry of Berks and diocese of Oxford; the Thame branch of the Great Western railway passes through and the branch crosses the river here over a bridge of three arches. The church of St. Swithin, built and consecrated in 1828, is a small edifice of stone in the Norman style, consisting of nave and a western bell-cote containing one bell and has been renovated. There are 80 sittings. In the garden of the manor house are some remains of the earlier church. The parishes of Kennington and Radley were again reunited in August, 1904, the church of the former undergoing thorough restoration. The register dates from the year 1829. The living is a vicarage, yearly value £170, in the gift of All Souls College, Oxford, and held since 1904 by the Rev. Charles B. Longland M.A. of Worcester College, Oxford, who is also vicar of Radley, where he resides. Edgar Norton Disney B.A. oxon. of The Hyde, Ingatestone, Essex, is lord of the manor and chief landowner. Egrove Farm, by Local Government Board Order 18,177, has been transferred from Radley; it is about a mile northwest of the village and commands a magnificent view of Oxford and the surrounding country; the celebrated picture of Oxford, by J. M. W. Turner R.A. is supposed to have been taken from this spot. The soil is principally stone brash, resting on the limestone. The crops are grain in succession. The area is 430 acres; the population in 1911 was 281.

Parish Clerk, George Godfrey.

Letters arrive at 8.15 a.m. & 3.30 p.m. through Oxford, which is the nearest money order & telegraph office

The WALL LETTER Box is cleared at 10.55 a.m. & 6.20 p.m. & sundays at 9.55 a.m

National School, built in 1803 & rebuilt in 1892 at a cost of over £200, for 36 children; average attendance, 24; Mrs. Alice King, mistress

PRIVATE RESIDENTS.

Andrews James, Haventhorpe
Arnold George, River view
Back Charles, St. Clare
Bishop Thomas, Castle croft
Brooks Walter Tyrrell M.A., M.B
Candy Walter Yeoman, Nettleham
Carter John Francis, 2 Alexandra villas
Chamberlain William, Fairfield
Charlton George, Mona cottage

Chatwell Archer William, The Cottage, Bagley wood
Collier William M.A., M.D
Cross Edward
Dines Horace Grant, Ringwood
Doman Walter Charles, Ellenglade
Draper Alfred, Lynton
Dunn John, Stellenbosch
Faulkner William, Ingledene
Gibbs Arthur Albert, Rose villa

Glover James, Woodlands
Harvey Owen
Hewer Frederick, Ava cottage
Kimber Henry
King Percival Henry, The Hawthorns
Kirk William, Trevely
Luckett Frank, Châlet
Lysaght Rev. Hon. Hy.M.A. The Bungalow
Phillips Harry, Ingleside
Pryer Louis Henley, Belinda cottage
Saunders Maurice Edwd. 3 Alexandra vils
Scarrott John, Glengarry
Silvester George James, The Hut
Simkins Frederick William, The Hollies
Smith Albert William, Underwood
Spender E
Steventon Albert, Scripplea villas
Streaks Arnold Cuthbert, Thames view
Weller John Percival, Lyndhurst

COMMERCIAL.

Allen Thomas, general dealer
Avery Arthur Edwin, travelling draper
Charlton Harry, dairy, Underwood
Cox Thomas, Radley College laundry
Faulkner Alfred James, builder & contractr
Faulkner F. (Mrs.), general stores
Godfrey George, parish clerk
King James Francis, farmer, Egrove farm
Mundy Mrs. farmer, Manor House farm
Oxford University Golf House & Club (Joseph William Gynes, sec. ; Charles H. Gibson, professional ; Henry Bodimeade, resident steward)
Slay Miss, laundress, The Cottage
Walker Alfred William, The Tandem P.H
Weller John Percival, builder, Lyndhurst

Kellys Directory 1913. (Reed Information Systems)

SECTION THREE
The Parish

Beating the Bounds on May 16th, 1936 of the New Parish of Kennington, created 1st April 1936.

Those taking part were: Mr Barker, Mrs Burton, Messrs Archie Burton, Tom Carter, Horace Chasney, Dick Cumpston, Mrs Elston, Messrs Cyril Gardiner, A M Grundy, Sam Grundy on the extreme left, Higgs, G Holmes, Miss Jones, Messrs Jack E Lloyd, W G Parker, J Porter, Monty Robinson, George Simpson, H Smith, Stanbridge, W Upton, E Viner, Misses Sheila Elston, Joan Lord (centre in black beret), Betty Chasney, Masters Doug Francis, Desmond Draper, Doug Macpherson, Dick Wallis, Ray Simpson, Eric Chasney, Ray Chasney. Radley College: Messrs P A Hannen, J L L Savill.

At this time Kennington was divided between two neighbouring parishes - South Hinksey to the north and Radley to the south. This division was roughly marked by a stream which ran down from Bagley Woods past Colley Wood, and the property known as The Lawn, down onto the Kennington Road. In 1974, following changes in county boundaries, Kennington was moved from Berkshire into Oxfordshire.

The 21st Birthday of the Parish Council in 1957, left to right: Mrs E Lightwood, Mr W Gray, Mrs G K Simpson, Mr H Dolman, Mr G K Simpson, Mr G Poole, Mr H S Rowles, Mr R Gibbons, Mrs H S Rowles, Mr H Rockall.   George Simpson is holding the silver trowel which had been used by Mrs Liddiard, the vicar's wife, to lay the foundation stone of the New Village Hall which was opened in 1940.

The 21st Parish Birthday Cake was cut by the three members with the longest service on the committee, left to right, Mrs E Burton, Mrs H S Rowles and Miss E Rockall, watched by Mr George K Simpson, chairman of the Kennington Village Hall Management Committee.

The Parish Council in 1957 standing on the steps of the Village Hall. Left to right back row: Rev Stuart Davies, L F 'Sam' Radford Treasurer of Abingdon Rural District Council, –, –, Tom Brooks, Reg Jackson, Cyril Pearce, Bill Gray, –, A C Cope, Mrs Westlake, Miss Davenport, Mrs Butler, Monty Robinson. Middle section: Howard Cornish chairman of Abingdon RDC, Mr Kirk, Mr Minchen, Mr Hegarty, George Simpson, Ted Perkins, –. Front row: Mr Hunt, Mrs Simpson, Mrs Burton, Mr Rowles.

George Simpson was born in 1895. He was awarded the MBE for his voluntary services to Kennington. He was the first clerk to Kennington Parish Council and later its Chairman. During the war he was billeting officer for the large number of evacuees who were sent to Kennington. Seen here in November 1981 presenting a Chairman's Badge of Office to Hettie Perkins, the Chairman. Simpsons Way is named after Mr George Simpson, and Perkins after Hettie Perkins.

Hettie Perkins, nee Adams, was born on 1st October 1909 in Hackney, London. She came to Kennington in 1956, moving into a new house in Bagley Close. Hettie quickly joined the Women's Institute and was elected as the representative on the Kennington Village Hall committee. In her own words 'if you want to find out anything you've got to be in it', a sentiment which resulted in her serving on the Parish Council for many years, retiring in May 1991.

Reg Jackson c1945. The Jackson family lived at 1 Sandford Lane, a property called Montlhery, after a racing track in Europe. This reflected Mr Jackson's life long interest in motor racing. He was associated with MGs at Abingdon for many years. Jackson Drive is named after Mr Jackson.

The Village Hall

The original village hall, known as the Memorial Hall, stood adjacent to 165 Kennington Road, directly opposite the bottom of Edward Road, seen here on the right hand side.

This was an ex-Army hut, approximately 80 foot long and 18 foot wide, bought and erected by ex-service men as a Memorial Hall. The first minutes of the Memorial Hall committee are dated 7 November 1924, when the chairman was Capt. R E Spender. In 1935 the committee agreed that 25% of the profits from the Memorial Hall should be allocated to a New Hall fund and a sub-committee, comprising Messrs Simpson, Grundy, Rowles, Brand, J Gibbons, Mrs Walters and Miss Rockhall, was formed to organise fundraising towards the cost of the new Village Hall. At the outbreak of war *the Memorial Hall was used in connection with evacuation work, for meetings in connection with billeting, and as a reception station during the evacuation of children to Kennington. The hall has also been used as a school for the evacuees.'* The new Village Hall was completed during 1940 and, in 1944, the Memorial Hall building was sold for £55. The site was sold several years later to a Mr F Pratley of 83 Kennington Road, for £145, and this transaction was completed on 17 January 1949. Total funds of £195 15 2 were realised and put towards the extension of the Kennington Village Hall.

A collection of local notables in front of the Memorial Hall, probably in the early 1920s. No doubt some of these gentlemen were the very same ex-service men who had erected the hall. Most of the men are wearing rosettes or lapel badges and one wonders what the occasion might have been. The only people identified are Jack East front row 3rd from left, and Mr Ewer far right in the back row. The Rev Marcon is in the centre. Bert Rockall and Archie Burton are also in the group.

The cowsheds on the left and the barn on the right in 1935 before conversion into club rooms and the new village hall during 1939. Despite the outbreak of the war, building continued as premises were required for war-time purposes. The village hall was opened on 6th June 1940 and the boys club moved to their new premises. *'We used to hang up flags, bunting all round, sweep down the cobwebs and sweep the concrete floor so we could have dances in there.'*

The village hall during the 1950s, as it is remembered by most villagers. The person in front is believed to be Mrs Phyllis Woodley, who was secretary and caretaker of the village hall for many years.

Regular whist drives were held in the hall for the 'Over 70s'. This is one of the first ones held during the early 1950s. Left to right facing: Sarah Trinder, Martha Howard, Mr Viner, –, Percy Horton. Front row: Mr Bridgeman, Mr Rowles, Jack Godfrey, George Hughes, Percy King, Mr Kirk. The lady in the hat, at the end of the table, is Mrs Cumsden.

The Village Hall during demolition in 1987.

The site being prepared for the new building. The social club is on the left hand side and behind is the original youth club.

The original youth club consisted of wartime wooden huts that had been dismantled and rebuilt by the boys themselves. It took almost a year to put down a concrete foundation. Jordan Hall, named after Cyril Jordan the Kennington builder, was erected at the back of the site. The wooden hut was replaced by extending Jordan Hall.

The Tandem

The Tandem in the 1920s, with a Morland brewery dray on the right hand side.

The Tandem was formerly known as The Fish Inn and has been part of village life since at least the 18th century. In the public bar is a stone bearing the date 1770 and the initials T.W., standing for Timothy West, a builder, who carried out alterations or repairs in that year.

In the Inclosure Award of 1802 the property is called The Fish and it is not known for certain when the name was changed. The reason for the change, however, would appear to be associated with the sporting habits of Oxford students who were forbidden to drive their horses 'in tandem' within the City. It became fashionable to drive out from Oxford with only one horse and harness a second horse from the stables at the inn, which was, of course, within Berkshire.

The Tandem in the 1930s.

The landlord from 1892 was Alfred 'Hooky' Walker who remained for over 30 years. After his death in 1921 Mrs Walker continued for a few years. Horace Chasney was landlord from March 1924, with his wife, Lilian. *'There was always a good garden trade. We catered for boating parties and provided teas. Boats used to pull in down by the gate at the bottom. There was a little bridge as well by that stream and at one time you could punt right up to what we called the old stile, just at the bottom of the railway bridge. They filled the stream in when the pylons were put up down there during the war.'*

The Tandem 1932 with Bob Simpson on the left and George Glynn on the right. Note the boundary wall and the original line of the road.

A large sign on the side of the Tandem Cottage advertised the Tandem facilities. During the 1935 Jubilee celebrations this old carriage, belonging to the Allen family, caused a lot of interest. Top left to right: Ray Chasney, Norman Chasney, Joan Godfrey, Thelma Croft. Seated: June Chasney, Daphne Wacknell. Front: Eric Chasney, Les Wacknell, Betty Chasney.

The Tandem was rebuilt in 1939 when the thatch was removed and the roof was tiled. Horace Chasney had started a car hire business before the war which was virtually the only taxi service in Kennington.

Horace Chasney retired in June 1958, following the death of his wife, Lilian in February. Ray Chasney, with his wife Doris, took over the Tandem, thus maintaining a family tradition that would last 58 years. Left to right: Betty Chasney, Frank Tomlin, Horace Chasney, Larry Richens, Mr Milton the butcher.

The Tandem Cottages soon to be demolished. During the war years the cottages were occupied by Mrs Cumsden, Mrs Godfrey, Mr and Mrs Wacknell, and another Mrs Cumsden. Note the curve of the road at this time. Following the demolition of the cottages, and the Sunday School opposite in 1953, the road was straightened and a grass verge in front of The Tandem is the original line of the earlier road. (Photograph by R H G Simpson)

Demolition of The Tandem Cottages c1947. Horace Chasney is standing on the wall. New properties were erected on this site; a house at the rear occupied by Mr Ray Chasney and an extension to the old barn which was used as a bank at one time, later a bookmakers, but is currently closed. Mrs Gwen Trinder and her two children, George and Jean, are on the far side, the lady in front is unknown.

An aerial view showing the Tandem middle right and the village hall bottom right.

A Bar Billiards team from the Tandem in the late 1970s. Left to right: Geoff Organ, Ray Chasney landlord, Brian Evans, Jim Allen, George Cox. The Tandem always had a very strong bar billiards team, in which the landlord, Ray Chasney, was a leading player.

Ray and Doris Chasney retired as landlords in October 1982, ending a family association as publicans lasting fifty eight years. Left to right: Doris Chasney, Ray Chasney, Uncle Dick Chasney, June Poole nee Chasney, Audrey Chasney, Norman Chasney.

Schooling

The Old Sunday School during the war, with Mr Edward Viner of 196 Upper Road. The sign above the door reads 'County Library'.

Let into the wall in front of the Kennington Medical Centre is a modern stone slab inscribed *'Sunday School 1809'*. The original date had been carved into a long piece of oak, above the door, but disappeared when the road was widened during the 1950s. This small building, probably the first school building in Kennington, may well have been built by Sir George Bowyer, 2nd Baronet. The building was not included in the 1913 estate sale, but the plot of land, Lot 20, known then as The Orchard, in the corner of which it stood, was sold as a *'valuable building site'*.

In 1916 a small piece of land at the rear of the Sunday School was conveyed to the Vicar, the Rev C B Longland, by Miss K E Hodgkins, and in 1919 Mr Disney made a Deed of Gift to him of the School itself. The land and the 1809 building was conveyed by the Vicar to the Oxford Diocesan Board in November 1919, at which time the building was called *'the Parish Reading Room (formerly the old Sunday School)'* and was used as a library, *'opened every Friday afternoon by Miss Mundy.'*

In May 1939 Berkshire County Council made an offer of £125 for the old School building which was declined. In 1952 the council wished to widen the road and offered £225. The surveyor at that time reported that the building was a single-storey stone and slated building whose floor space was 18ft 10ins by 15ft 11ins; the frontage to the road was 29ft and the total area about 196 square yards. There was a timber floor, gas laid on, and the boundary walls were in bad condition. Up to 1948 it had been used as a Sunday School and had since been used for storage and occasional parochial purposes. In October 1953 the building, seen here on the right hand side, passed to the Berkshire County Council and was demolished in 1954. (R H G Simpson)

In 1889 Colonel E J Disney granted to the Minister and Churchwardens of Kennington the site of the present school, being 100ft by 109 ft. Kellys Directory

for 1893 records that the new school, Kennington National School, for 45 children opened on 15 September 1890 at a cost of £200. The school building was only slightly larger than the original Sunday School building, being 24ft by 18ft. *'I remember the cherry tree up at the top and every spring some of the older boys would pick the cherries and they used to throw them down and we all used to cluster round and see how many we could catch.'*

In 1906 the name of the school was changed to Radley Kennington National School and it was re-roofed. This photograph of 1906 includes Flo and Wynn Webb (both marked with a cross). Wynn is the younger, blond girl in the centre; the two sisters never married. Mrs King, the teacher, is on the right hand side. She resigned in 1915 after 18½ years service.

The Avenue in 1912, believed to have been taken near the school, looking towards Radley. It is reported that the original trees in the Avenue had been planted to commemorate the Battle of Trafalgar in 1805. *'There were no paths, only a bit of a small path on one side and the grass verges. It was a lovely avenue of trees which was known as the Radley Road. There was an old chap – Old Man Cudd – used to sweep all these leaves up. He had a beard and was a typical Berkshire man.'*

A new classroom was built in 1914 which enlarged the capacity of the buildings to take 28 infants and 42 older children. Mrs King was succeeded in 1915 by Miss Elsie Beatrice Mundy, one of the daughters of Job Mundy. *'Sally' Mundy lived on the main road — a property which is now a nursing home, Mon Choisie.* After World War I the numbers increased considerably, reaching 48 in October 1919. Miss Mundy's salary in 1921 was £244 15sh 0d per annum, and she was allowed a second assistant

Kennington School 1930, left to right back row: –, –, –, Reggie Rowles, –, Jack Peedell, Sylvia Horrell, Heather Macpherson. Middle row: Arthur Berry, Betty Berry in front, Len Peedell, Cyril Peedell, –, –, –, Ethel Spracklen?. Front row: Les Jackman, –, –, Wilf Peedell, Jack Francis, –, Barbara Wallis. *'We always wore boots and the place was filthy inside. Mrs Gibbons was the caretaker, a very old fashioned lady, used to wear her skirts right down to her ankles and rode an upright bike.'*

Further expansion took place in 1935 with the building of a new classroom for 40 children at a cost of about £475. On 2 July 1935 Mrs Emily Copp, widow of John Copp of the Manor House, sold to the Vicar and Churchwardens land for use as a playground, at a cost of £35. This was immediately behind the existing school and measured 100ft x 50ft.

Miss Mundy resigned through ill health at the end of September 1936, after 21 years service. Her successor was Miss A R Drew. Electric lighting was installed in 1938. By September 1939 the number of pupils had risen to 105 plus 13 evacuees.

Because of the increased numbers during the war years, it was necessary for some classes to be held in the old Memorial Hall, and in the new Village Hall, which had been opened on 6 June 1940. The new Village Hall continued to be used for teaching for a further 15 years.

In October 1943 additional land was acquired for a playground, 160ft square, immediately behind the existing playground, at a cost of £676. At this time the school was known as Kennington Church of England Junior School and the number on roll in April 1943 was 122. Miss Drew resigned during that year, and Mrs C G Byford succeeded her on 8 January 1945. Because of shortage of space 78 children were being taught in the school and 42 in the Village Hall.

Kennington School April 1948. Left to right back row: Heather Middleton, Janet Matthews, Pauline Green, Anne Smith, Gillian Butler. Middle: Anita Ball, Valerie Song, Janet Davis, Victor Gregory, Neville Powell, Richard Lord, Peter Ball, David Hackett, Christine Clark, –, Pam Kearsey. Next row: Beryl Reid, Wanda Wheel, Audrey Kerby. Front: Cliff Rogers, Michael Cox, –, Dennis Forster, –, Michael Simms, Billy Holcroft, –.

Kennington School 1953/54. Left to right back row: Pat Tait, Muriel Talboys, Jennifer Humphries, Pat Woodley, Irene Morris, Hazel Kirby, Jennifer Nash. Next row: Julie Shaw, Jean Kirby, Ann Verney, Rodney Pitt, Roger Prior, Bobby Purvey, Roy Faulkner, Paul Britton, Chris Spencer, –, Elizabeth Hall, Felicity Walkington, Jennifer Collis. Next row: Maurita Hebborn, Susan Boare, Maureen Hebborn, Joyce Ball, Rosemary Pitter, Angerina Walker, Elizabeth Clinkard, Sonia Rowles, Shirley Barson, Sally Williamson. Front row: Michael Keep, Steven Lord, Dennis Westell, Peter Laukes, R Janes, Paul Treviss, William Beyer.

In 1947 the question of a new school was under discussion, at an estimated cost of £40,000. Half this cost would need to be raised if the school were to remain a Church school. In February 1952 the Vicar advised the school managers that funding of £33,200 would have to be found for the new building. This was an impossible amount of money to find; consequently the school was transferred to the Berkshire Education Committee at the end of June 1952.

A new block of three classrooms was ready for occupation by 1955, at which time 97 children were still being taught in the Village Hall. These children transferred to the new classrooms, which were heated by coke stoves and equipped with cloakrooms, lavatories and washing provisions. The remaining 87 children remained in the three small rooms in the old building. The first school secretary was appointed on 1 August 1955.

Kennington School Reception Class in 1954, left to right back row: David Butler, Leslie —, Malcolm —, Rosemary Stanley, David Jones, Ann —, Carl —, Susan Jones, Mark Vigor. Seated: —, —, —, Gillian Perkins, Janet James, Marion Bellerby. On ground: Terry Brookes, Christopher Dunlop, Jean Webb?, Sandra Lawrence?, Linda Hamlet, Susan Cornell, Anthony Barnes, Peter Cornell. The teacher is Miss Franklin, reception class teacher for many years.

The Reception Class in 1955, left to right back row: Richard?-, David Villeboys, D Jones, —, Neville Westlake, Nicola Smith, Jean-, —, —, —, David Hartigan, —. Seated: —, —, —, Sandra Lawrence, —, Wendy Villeboys, Jeanette Heggerty. Front row: Dennis Shaw, Martin Tasker, —Barnes, Chris Thompson, John Butler, David-, John Goldsworthy, —, John Hamlet, Christopher Dunlop.

1956 Reception Class at the Village Hall. Left to right back row: −, Ann Rosser, −, Odette Holt, Bernard Workman, −, −, −. Seated: −, −, −, Miss Franklin, −, −, Anita James?. Front row: Rodney Giddings, −, David Shelton, Robert Betteridge, Andrew Boult, −, John Workman. Kennington's population expanded rapidly in the 1950s and in April 1956 it was necessary for 60 younger infants to return to the Village Hall. On 10 January 1957 a further block of four classrooms was started and on 20 December the infants were moved back to the school from the Village Hall.

Kennington School Christmas Concert held in the Village Hall, possibly 1958.

Kennington School 1953, left to right back row: Rolland Godfrey, Mary Loukes, Ian MacDonald, Margaret Francis, Keith Miles, Susan Pratley, Alan Cusden, Faye Mitchell, Alan Ball. Seated: Kenny Kirby, Richard Wallington, Suzanne Yeates, Hazel Boare, —, Dinah Wallington, Gill Berry, Kathleen Kirby, Susan Beyer, John Holcroft, Neil Gatley. In front: David Haggerty, —, —, Rex Workman, Peter Song, Paul Clarke, Chris Spragg.

Kennington School 1961, left to right back row: Susan Cousins, Marianne Thompson, Jane Hicks, —, —, —, Angela Baker. Next row: Sean Mills, Roy Tasker, Martin Adams, —, Mark Lemmon, Geoffrey Cummings, —, Timothy Hallum. Next row: —, Elizabeth Finch, Paula Dickenson, —, Susan Wilde, —, Francis Drake, Judith Swanson, —, Karen Rogers, Jennifer Hitchen. Front row: Robert Ferriman, Adrian Ware, David Ainsley, —, Jane Amor, Mark Osborn, Stuart Giles, Andrew Dixon, Paul Pratley.

Junior IA Class 1961/62. Left to right back row: Helen Woods, Christine Grant-Robertson, Diana Thorpe, Janet Whitehouse, Susan Kerby, Pauline Cox, Hilary Perkins, Kathleen Sharpe. Next row: David Taylor?, Stuart Almond, Oliver Sutton, —, Paul Swan?, Lincoln Fishpool, Robert-, Christopher Amor, Neil Hartigan, Derek Rodgers, Russell Hallam. Next row: Angela Mills, Judith Ainsley, Jane Goodey, Miss East or Mrs Rumary, Penelope Townsend, Jane House, Doreen Lovett. Front row: Clive Harold, Peter Kubat, —, Mark Lemmon, Victor Morris, Keith —, Martin Pether, —, Andy Barnes?

Junior 2A Class 1962/63. Left to right back row: Susan Vaughan, Joy Rosser, Janet Whitehouse, Susan Kerby, Christine Grant-Robertson, Diana Thorpe, Helen Woods. Next row: Graham Canning?, Robert-, Paul Swan?, Lincoln Fishpool, Oliver Sutton, Mark Lemmon, Russell Hallam, Christopher Amor, Derek Rodgers, Peter Kubat, John Hamlet. Next row: Pauline Cox, Hilary Perkins, Penelope Townsend, Jane House, Mrs Brenda Cowlett, Susan Archer, Angela Mills, Jane Goodey, Doreen Lovett, Judith Ainsley. Front row: Martin Pether?, David Taylor?, Stuart Almond, Neil Hartigan, Clive Harold, —, Keith-, Victor Morris, —, —.

Brownies and Guides

The 1st Kennington Brownies in 1936, outside the guide hut in Upper Road. Miss Edith Gandy is the tall lady at the back, with her assistant Miss Spracklen on her right. Left to right back row: Esther Goddard, Brenda Thompson, Ruth Broomfield, Janet Arkell, Muriel Villebois. Middle row: Sylvia Wilson, Daphne Hadland, -, Sylvia Theobald, Sheila Elston. In front: Hazel Jackson, Betty Chasney.

The 1st Kennington Brownies were started by Miss Edith Gandy in 1929, when she established both a guide company and a brownie pack. The meeting place was always called the 'guide hut', but was in fact a brick built hall, *'with the barest of essentials - no toilets, no running water, a wooden floor and one electric heater'*. The Brownies would meet every Saturday morning, paying a subscription of one penny. Mrs M E Smith, neé Spracklen, of 200 Upper Road was Miss Gandy's assistant in 1935, but was called up for navy service in the war. During the war years Miss Gandy changed the guide hut into a bungalow, to prevent it being taken over by the army as a storage depot. The pack closed in 1943 when Miss Gandy started work at the Post Office.

1943 1st Kennington Guide Company, outside Guide H.Q. This building stood near the entrance to the Methodist Church, and the land surrounding it was owned by Miss Gandy. The group includes: Ruth Broomfield, Heather Macpherson, Sylvia Theobald, Margaret Thomas, Minnie Thomas (evacuee), Phyllis Kimber, Margaret Finch, Gill Rowles, Valerie Humphries, Marjory Woodward, Audrey Purvey, Ann Picking, Lucy Broomfield, Pamela Cox, Sally Underwood, Wendy Jackson, Jean Cox, Joan Beesley, Pat Harris, Margaret Beyer, — Baskerville.

Wings for Victory parade in April 1943.   Every organisation participated, marching around the village. These guides are just passing 'Cumberford' at 135 Kennington Road, the bungalow home of the Theobald family. Left to right: Sylvia Theobald, -, Margaret Thomas, Janet Arkell, Miss Edith Gandy, Gwyneth Thomas. *There were allotments in the vicarage grounds during the war and the guides were supposed to dig and produce vegetables for victory. Mrs Liddiard, the vicar's wife, brought out lemonade - she was a large gushing sort of lady. We also used to collect stems out of batteries - the carbon rods, and waste paper which had to be taken down to Warburtons in Oxford, pushed on a hand barrow'.*

Whitsun Church Parade for the 1st Kennington Guides in 1947. Left to right back row: Mary Lord, Nancy Harvey, Wendy Jackson, Joan Benwell, Ann Lawrence, Sylvia Theobald, Gillian Smith. Middle row: Ann Picking, Jean Cox, Valerie Humphries, Pat Cook, Joan Giles, Sue Collett. Front row: Sylvia Kirby, Margaret Beyer, Shirley Moffat, Sally Underwood.

1st Kennington Brownies outside the Village Hall in 1952, with Mrs Talboys.

Brownies were started up again in 1951 under Jill Bond, nee Rowles, of 70 Meadowview Road, with Mrs Talboys. The Pack closed again in 1956. In 1959 it was started by Mrs Zarachy and the Pack grew from nine to twenty-four girls — meeting in Mrs Zarachy's garden at 110 Poplar Grove, before moving to St Swithun's Hall, then to the Scout Hut. A 2nd Brownie Pack was started by Rene Gower in 1963, and a 3rd Pack by Jill Price in 1973.

1st Kennington Guides in July 1950. Left to right: Ann Crutch, Noni Wallington, Sally Underwood, Shirley Moffat, Sylvia Rivers, Joan Richings, Ann Berry, Lorraine Yates, -, Janet Theobald, Pam Hewer. Front: Susan Williamson, Glenys Jones.

Armistice Day Parade 1961. Susanna Wykes is carrying the colours, escorted by Ann Baker, Jennifer Morris, Susan Cornell and Linda Hamlet. The Village Hall is in the background.

War Years

The 1st Berkshire (Abingdon) Local Defence Volunteers was renamed the Home Guard in July 1940. The Battalion Commander was Lt Col S T Austin, second in command Major J S Gowring, Captain O H M Sturges serving as Adjutant to the Battalion, Lt A T Baskerville was appointed as Transport Officer. Battalion strength was divided amongst 40 platoons. Kennington (No 11 Platoon) was part of C Company, the other platoons being No 9 (Hinksey), No 10 (Cumnor) and No 12 (Boars Hills).

Left to right back row: −, −, −, G Hughes, −, −, L Howes, −, J Hughes, −, H Cox, Freddie Godfrey, M Saunders, −. Next row: Frank Miles, Charlie Theobald, Harry Doman, −, −, Jack Peedell snr, Jack Godfrey, −, George Poole, Jack Kerby, Tommy Tait, Mr Myers, Cyril Peedell, R Hughes, −, Dr Harrison. Next row: −, Walt Trinder, Bert Rockall, Mr Rowles, A Elston, A Livsey, −, Lt Smith, A Baskerville, George Hughes, Mr Streakes, F Marsh, Monty Robinson, Bill Gray. Front row: −, Maurice Farr, −, Jack Gibbons, −, Eric Chasney, Ted Dowse snr, Mr Maidon.

A procession through the village during Salute the Soldier Week in June 1944. This photograph was taken from the top of Edward Road, along Upper Road towards Kenville Road. (Photograph by R H G Simpson)

Saluting the flag following the Salute the Soldier procession in 1944. Every village organisation was represented during these parades and took an active part in the fundraising to support the armed forces. (photograph by R H G Simpson)

Civil defence photograph in the 1940s, taken in the Tandem car park. Left to right back row: Horace Walker, Mr Wiggins, Sherwin, George Shorter, A Walton, Mrs Russell from Hinksey Hill, Alf Allsworth, Percy Mills, Sam Chandler, Cook, Titchener, –, Talboys. Middle row: Reg Jackson, Mr Tuffrey, Mr Bint, Alan Green, Miss C Brown church organist, Mrs Knight, Mrs Broomfield, Miss Hall, Mrs Gwen Fensome, Mrs Barnes, Mrs Minchin, Sid Knight, Norman Uzzell. Front row: Ms Kersey, Miss Arkell, Mrs Francis, Miss Olive Hortin, Joan Godfrey, Mr Kirk, Mr Ewers, Mrs Maiden, Julie Francis, Nora Honey, Heather Macpherson, Mrs V Harrison.

Following the First World War, a War Memorial was erected on the corner of Cow Lane, next to the church, seen here c1920. William Trinder is standing 5th from the left in the right hand group, and his sister Mary is standing 4th from the left in the left hand group. The Trinder family lived at Anglebee, 38 Bagley Wood Road. The thatched cottage on the left was occupied by 'Man' Gould.

The War Memorial in its original position next to the church. Following the Second World War several residents formed the Kennington Ex-Services Association, with a membership fee of half a crown (2sh 6d) a year. This provided funds for any member who was sick. The Association held an annual remembrance dinner on the Friday before Armistice Sunday. Eventually membership dwindled and any remaining funds were handed to the parish council to maintain the war memorial and help provide the annual poppy wreath.

Looking north along Kennington Lane from the corner of the church, pre-war. The war memorial can be seen behind the stone pillar on the right. The white cottage in the centre is Wych-Elm Cottage, now known as The Onion Patch. The large walnut tree on the left of the photograph stood opposite Jasmine Cottage and was 'guarded' by 'Jinny' Steptoe.

The War Memorial was moved across the road to its present site c1958, as part of the continuing road improvement and re-alignment from the Tandem corner. The names recorded on the memorial are: 1914-18 war:

M H Collier	C Gibbons,
G S King	P East,
G Finney	G R Godfrey,
H Charlton	H G Dines,
E Pryer	E J Wright,
F J Godfrey	W T Underwood.

1939-45 war:

D Bint	W Gobey
C H Bowley	A Kirk
W R Evers	S H Trinder

The Memorial Field c1960
(Photograph by Mrs W Spray)

At the end of the Second World War six Kennington families had been bereaved, losing their husbands or sons in active service. At this time the population of Kennington was some 1,600. Mrs Sarah Kirk, herself having lost a son, had the idea of acquiring the Field as a memorial to the six who had lost their lives in the War, which was to be left in its natural state for posterity

The Field was 12.26 acres, and purchased for a total cost of £1,000. £528 was raised by house to house collections, raffles, sale of work, a fete and a collection at Thanksgiving services, plus a few other donations. The Oxford Preservation Trust agreed to pay the outstanding cost, and deeds were conveyed on 21st December 1946, between William Dockar-Drysdale of Wick Hall Estates Ltd and the Oxford Preservation Trust. The Oxford architect and artist, Mr Thomas Rayson, was consulted for the design of the gates and the inscription. (Extracted from *The Kennington Memorial Field* by Mrs W Spray.)

Since 1931 the Field had been tenanted by Mr George Woodley, a Radley farmer, who grazed sheep and heifers there. In 1961 his son, Harold Woodley, took over the tenancy to graze steers, and also maintained the fences, pasture and hedges.

In 1950 the Oxford Mail reported that a speedway cycle track and regular gymkhanas would not be allowed, in accordance with the covenants which provided that the Field would remain 'open space for all time'.

Kennington Cold Store staff in 1947, left to right back row: Mr Johnson chief engineer, Mr East manager who lived in Poplar Grove, Mr Aitken Reading manager, Mr Hawkins chief clerk, Mr Young of Reading. Middle row: Mr Farrell of Reading branch, Miss Muriel Villebois, Mr Spearing, Mrs Benwell, Mr Wilkson, Mr Wareham foreman of the loading bay.

Muriel Villebois and Sheila Elston outside the Cold Store building in 1946.

In July 1942 a Ministry of Food cold store was opened at Kennington and was situated south of the Cow Lane railway crossing.

The store was provided with its own railway sidings which were reached from the down goods line, the connection being controlled from the nearby Sandford Box. The frozen carcasses were delivered to the cold store using both road and rail, and subsequently distributed by road. It was owned by the International Cold Storage Company, controlled by the Ministry of Food, and supplied all the bases, army and airforce, with meat. The men on the loading bank had to unload the rail carriages, check the delivery and put it into store in the big freezer rooms which were extremely cold. The men wore only leather jerkins against the grease and dirt. When the Americans came into the war they had an office in the cold store building and meat was supplied to the American base at Upper Heyford.

'There was a road right down to the big gates at the top and into the entrance, and three gatemen were employed working six hour shifts. It was a very stark building with a wire fence all around. After the war we stored margarine, apples etc. It was very cold in the offices, just one pipe going round the wall and one small electric fire.' The rail connection was removed on 28 June 1969 and the cold store itself was demolished during the mid 1980s to allow for housing development, now Otters Reach.

VE Day Party 1945, held to celebrate Victory in Europe. This was held in Mr and Mrs Lawrence's front garden at 192 The Avenue. 1 Peter Clarkson, 2 Jimmy Clarkson, 5 Peter Ball?, 10 Marian Lawrence, 11 Jennifer Humphreys, 13 Jean Welsley, 17 Rhona Parker, 18 Gerald Fountain, 19 Christine Fountain, 20 Barry Jackson, 21 Mary Lord, 22 Robert Jones, 23 Norman Bowden, 24 Peter Fountain (as a gollywog), 25 Nonnie Wallington, 26 Ann Lawrence, 30 Sue Jackson, 32 Frankie Titchener, 37 Kenneth Crutch, 38 Wendy Jackson, 39 Sue Collett, 40 Bruce Crozier, 41 David Brown, 42 Pat Cook, 44 Joan Benwell, 46 Arthur Rickman.

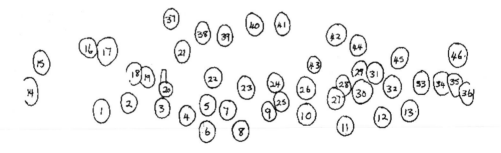

Key to above

Celebrations and Events

The Silver Jubilee of King George V and Queen Mary in 1935 was cause for celebration throughout the United Kingdom. At Kennington the children showed their patriotic colours. Left to right: Isaac Bunce, Peter Finch, Norman Chasney, June Chasney, Beryl Kerby, Betty March, Brenda Allen, Tony Taylor. Gladys Theobald recalled *'people decorated Kennington with red, white and blue, my brother-in-law put cocoa all over his face — I think he thought he was an Indian prince — and he took my patchwork quilt, put it round his shoulders and jumped on to an old carriage that belonged to the Allen family.'*

'Over in the meadows, just over the bridge at the back of the Tandem, they laid out a running track and had running races and a real gala there, a fete and everything for the kids. And on the river at night they had all the punts lit up.'

The Village Hall was naturally the centre of any celebration, including those for the 1953 Coronation of Queen Elizabeth II.

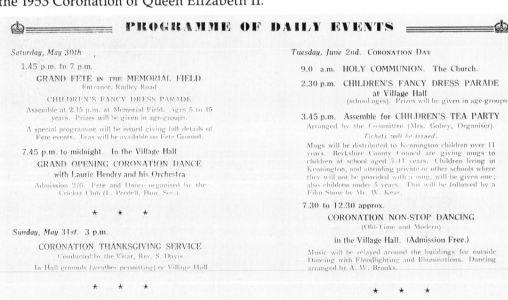

PROGRAMME OF DAILY EVENTS

Saturday, May 30th

1.45 p.m. to 7 p.m.

GRAND FETE IN THE MEMORIAL FIELD
Entrance, Radley Road

CHILDREN'S FANCY DRESS PARADE

Assemble at 2.15 p.m. at Memorial Field. Ages 5 to 15 years. Prizes will be given in age-groups.

A special programme will be issued giving full details of Fete events. Teas will be available on Fete Ground.

7.45 p.m. to midnight. In the Village Hall

GRAND OPENING CORONATION DANCE
with Laurie Hendry and his Orchestra

Admission 2/6. Fete and Dance organised by the Cricket Club (L. Peedell, Hon. Sec.).

★　★　★

Sunday, May 31st. 3 p.m.

CORONATION THANKSGIVING SERVICE
Conducted by the Vicar, Rev. S. Davis

In Hall grounds (weather permitting) or Village Hall

★　★　★

Monday, June 1st. 7 p.m.

FOLK DANCING DISPLAY
by members of the Junior School under the direction of Mrs. Hayes, to be followed by a

DISPLAY by the GIRLS' VENTURE CLUB
directed by Mrs. F. Day (Piano: Miss Brown)
on Playground fronting Club-Room (weather permitting), otherwise in the Village Hall

Tuesday, June 2nd. CORONATION DAY

9.0 a.m. HOLY COMMUNION. The Church.

2.30 p.m. CHILDREN'S FANCY DRESS PARADE
at Village Hall
(school ages). Prizes will be given in age-groups.

3.45 p.m. Assemble for CHILDREN'S TEA PARTY
Arranged by the Committee (Mrs. Gobey, Organiser).
Tickets will be issued.

Mugs will be distributed to Kennington children over 11 years. Berkshire County Council are giving mugs to children at school aged 5–11 years. Children living in Kennington, and attending private or other schools where they will not be provided with a mug, will be given one; also children under 5 years. This will be followed by a Film Show by Mr. W. Kear.

7.30 to 12.30 approx.

CORONATION NON-STOP DANCING
(Old-Time and Modern)

in the Village Hall. (Admission Free.)

Music will be relayed around the buildings for outside Dancing with Floodlighting and Illuminations. Dancing arranged by A. W. Brooks.

★　★　★

Wednesday, June 3rd

7.0 p.m.　CYCLE SPEEDWAY
Kennington Kestrels v. Rodbourne Rockets of Swindon
on the Village Hall Track (J. Lamper, Organiser).

7.30 p.m. CORONATION WHIST DRIVE
in the Village Hall, organised by the Whist Committee.
Admission 1/6.　Coronation Prizes.

Elizabeth R
1953

Coronation programme

A Coronation street party was held in Poplar Grove: the lady in the bath chair is Mrs Shaw. Left to right back row: Julie Shaw, Denis Shaw, Patsie Tait, Pat Woodley, −, Janet Shelton, −, Joan Allen. Front row: Kenny Shaw, Susan James, −, John Grant, (Jodie the dog), Jimmy James.

Frances Tait, Tilly Holt, Miss Maycock, Mrs Simms, Sheila Clark, Gill Butler, − Ainsley, − Ainsley, Mrs Giddings, −, Mrs Villebois.

Left back: Frances Tait, Mrs Caddick, Mrs Grant (back of), −, Mrs Tasker, Mrs Rivers. Children facing: Linda Hamlet, Janet Saunders, Malcolm Caddick, Kenny Saunders.

Poplar Grove 1953 Coronation celebrations. Left to right back row: Sheila Clarke, Joan Allen, Gill Butler, Maureen Duffey, Keith Dooley, Marcus Warner, Kenny Shaw, Bobby Purvey, Ron James. Next row: Julie Shaw in dark dress with white buttons, Phyllis Duffey, Sylvia Jordan, Patsie Villeboys, Becky Duffey, –, Tony Simms boy with twins, Mrs Workman, –. Next row: Jimmy James, John Grant, Christine James, Kenneth Saunders, Margaret Francis, Susan James, Jennifer Nash, Richard Simms, John Simms. Next row: Pat Woodley, Janet James, Mrs Betty James. Front row: –, Andy Chalmers, Malcolm Chalmers, Rex Workman, Rosemary Stanley, John Francis, Denise Kirby, Janet Butler, John Workman, Janet Saunders.

The other half of this party, left to right back row: Mrs Frances Tait, Mr Grant, Mrs Audrey Hartigan, Mrs Doris Francis, Beryl Reid, Gillian East, Mrs Giddings, Sheila Clark, Gill Butler, Patsie Tait, Joan Allen in front with white blouse, Maureen Duffey, Keith Dooley, Julie Shaw dark dress with white buttons, Phyllis Duffey, Kenneth Shaw. Middle row: Mrs Sylvia Rivers with Tony, Mrs Grant, –, Linda Hamlet, –,

Rodney Giddings, Stephen Giddings, Jimmy James, Christine James, Kenneth Saunders. Front row: Marlene Lovett, Brian Clark, David Ainsley, Judith Ainsley, –, David Butler, Pat Woodley behind, Andrew Chalmers, Malcolm Chalmers back of head, Rex Workman.

Miss Kennington 1947. Left to right: Mrs Humphries, Joan Holland, Sheila Elston, Sylvia Theobald, Margaret Thomas, Esther Goddard. *'We entered as a joke really. Mrs Rowles was organising this for one of the fetes and encouraged a few of us girls to enter. There were only six of us and whoever was supposed to judge did not turn up and they asked members of the band, from a neighbouring village, to judge.'*

May Day celebrations 4 May 1957. The May Queen this year was Jean Kerby, crowned by the Mayor and Mayoress of Abingdon, Councillor and Mrs C G Stow, with attendants Kathleen Kerby, Susan Monk and Susan Bore.

Kennington school dancers, at a fete in the grounds of St Veeps, 40 Bagley Wood Road c1935. The bonnets and sashes were made from coloured crepe paper. Left to right back row: Muriel Villebois, Joyce Kimber, Kathleen Arkell, Joan Godfrey, Nora Honey, Noel Broomfield, Bessy Parratt, Pamela Honey, Betty Chasney, Linda Allen, Beryl Sylvester. Front row: Diana Scarrott, Beryl Blakeman, Janet Arkell, Heather Macpherson, Sylvia Theobald, Sheila Elston, Betty Scarrott, Hazel Jackson, Ruth Broomfield.

Also at St Veeps c1935. The group includes, approximately left to right back row boys: Bill Kimber, —, Desmond Draper, Dick Wallis, Phillip Allen, —, Ray Simpson, —, Doug Francis, Douglas Macpherson, Spencer Rowles?. Next row: Ruth Broomfield, —, —, —, Tony Taylor, Ron Bowden, Janet Arkell, —, Sylvia Theobald, —, Peter Finch, Joan Lord, —, Tony Bennett, Muriel Villebois, Ray Chasney, —, Les Wacknell, Beryl Sylvester, Jo Beardsley, John Walters, Sheila Elston, —, —, —, —, —, Norman Chasney (3rd from right). Next row: —, —, —, Beryl Kirby, —, Dorothy Longthorpe, Ron Harris, —, —, —, Betty Pitter, —, Beryl Blakeman, —, Heather Macpherson, June Chasney, —Kirby, Joan Gray, —.

Kennington School of dancing at the Village Hall in the early 1940s. Left to right back row: −, −, −, Ann Willis (evacuee), Margaret Thomas, Sonia Pledge dancing teacher, Esther Goddard, Minnie Emery (evacuee), −, −, Barbara Pitts. Next row: −, −, −, −, Audrey Tuffrey, Pam Cox, Betty Pitter, −, Daphne Wacknell, Margaret Finch, Betty Godfrey. Next row: −, Vera Bowden, Hazel Brown, Brenda Allen, Beryl Kirby, Joan Gray, Janet Jefferies, Heather Macpherson, −, Nellie Regan. Front row: −, −, Wendy Jackson, Francis Goddard, −.

Sonia Pledge dance group in the car park of the Tandem during the 1940s. Left to right back row: Vera Bowden, Minnie Emery, −, Ann Willis, Heather Macpherson, Hazel Jackson, Sonia Pledge, Margaret Thomas, Esther Goddard, Janet Jefferies, −, Joan Gray, Hazel Brown. Next row: −, −, −, Audrey Tuffrey, Betty Pitter, Brenda Allen, Beryl Kirby. Next row: Barbara Pitts, Pam Cox, −, Wendy Jackson, Nellie Regan, Julie Regan, −. Babies at the front: −, −, Francis Goddard.

Sunday School group c1934, left to right back row: Muriel Villabois, Frances Godfrey, Mary Macpherson, Joyce Kimber, Beryl Sylvester. Middle row: –, Sheila Elston, –, Janet Arkell, –, Hazel Jackson, Betty Chasney, Sylvia Theobald. Front row: Heather Macpherson, –, –, Ruth Broomfield, Beryl Blakeman, June Chasney, Esther Goddard.

A group of country dancing girls behind the old Sunday School, at the 1953 Coronation celebrations. Left to right: Margaret Thomas?, Susan Jackson, Gillian Wyatt, Susanne Williamson, Maureen Petts, Mary Holcraft, Jill Spencer?, Sally Underwood, –, Beryl Reid, Sylvia Jordan, Janet Theobald, Pat-, Glenis Jones.

Recreation

Fund raising event in 1949, towards the cost of providing a sports field. This photograph was taken in Upper Road; the hedge behind marking the site of the Department of Forestry, what was to become Forest Side. Group includes: Maureen Hebborn, Maurita Hebborn, Kenny Saunders, Bette Mills, Doris Chasney, Ray Chasney, Audrey Acott, Brian Peedell, Fay Peedell.

'Years ago, us boys used to play football on a rough bit of ground up Little London, next to East's dairy. Later we had a piece of land down Egrove farm, where Templeton College was built. That also belonged to Mr East. We played in the field at the back of the old forestry nursery, now Forest Side. We had no pitch marked or nothing like that — just an open field. Our biggest thrill was to go down to Hinksey Step and play this team that Alf Jefferies arranged on the playing fields there. They had actual goal posts and the pitch was marked out. After the war one or two of us wanted somewhere to play football and cricket, and we realised that the land at the top of Playfield Road belonged to the parish, and would make a proper sport's ground. Not everyone was in favour of it at the time, but Kennington Sports Club was formed, and we had to raise all this money voluntarily to get something done about it, which we eventually did. We held fetes and dances, and once we hired a hurdy gurdy from Wantage and got up in fancy dress, and went round Kennington collecting'

A similar fund raising event includes Norman Chasney, George Butler, Ray Chasney, Beryl Reid, Maureen Petts, Janet Theobald, Pat Beyer, Mary Holcraft, Shirley Thomas, Sally Underwood, Len Peedell. The Playfield sports field was finally secured in 1951. *'The field was covered in stones and every Sunday a group of us would go up there and pick up buckets of stones and get the ground cleaned out. We had no pavilion up there, but a man in Upper Road had a wooden building, he sold it to us and we were allowed to take it down. We transported it up there ourselves, all done by voluntary labour.'*

In 1953 the Sports Club Committee issued a further appeal for funds, to enable the field to be levelled, grassed etc. and to be ready for the 1954 season. The committee at this time was: Len Peedell chairman, C L Scarrott Hon Sec., H Boore, M A Farr, G Butler, D G Butler, J C Smith, H Haytree, F J R Hall, L Field, W Worf, Mrs Worf, D Francis, H Underwood, Coun. W G Gray.

'The Village now possesses a piece of land some five acres in extent, situated between the Memorial Field on the south and the Well at Little London on the north side. This piece of land, while being no Kennington Oval, is capable of being transformed into a desirable playing field. Work is shortly to be started to achieve this. In April of this year the Parish Council convened a Public Meeting as a result of which the Kennington Sports Club has been formed to add yet another to the many thriving organisations in the Village. A Pavilion has been purchased, and is due to be erected on the field in the near future. Cricket, football, and tennis sections of the Sports Club are organised all with representatives on the Committee ready for the 1954 season, when we hope the Sports Ground will be ready for use. Membership of the Sports Club is open to all at an annual subscription of 2/6.'

KENNINGTON SPORTS CLUB
in conjunction with numerous other organisations, present a

FETE, WHIST DRIVE
AND
DANCE

to be held in the

Village Hall and Grounds, Kennington
SATURDAY, 26th SEPTEMBER, 1953
2 p.m. — Midnight
(in Aid of the Kennington Sports Ground)

PROGRAMME

1.30 to 2 p.m. — Men's Humourous Walking Race from Sandford Lane to the Village Hall. (subject to sufficient entries)   Entries to F. J. R. Hall

2 p.m. — Fancy Dress Parade (3 classes).   Class 1, up to 6 years; Class 2, 6 to 12 years; Class 3, 12 years and upwards including adults.
PRIZES—First 7/6, Second 5/-, Third 2/6
JUDGES—Mrs. J. M. Evens assisted by Mrs. Butterfield

Numerous Side-Shows including Bowls, Bingo, Darts, Skittles, Aunt Sally, Etc.
attended by members of Social Activities of the District

Ladies' Ankle Competition. Men's Knobbly Knees. Numerous Raffles
Refreshments from 3.30 onwards by W.I.

The Men's Club have kindly given permission to use Club Room in the afternoon

We Challenge YOU to Spot 'SPORTY' who will be in attendance at the Fete and give a Prize to the first person to correctly challenge 'SPORTY'
Buy a Ticket and Spot 'Sporty'

4 p.m. — CYCLE SPEEDWAY CHALLENGE MATCH
Kennington Kestrels v Wheatley Saints (arranged by Mr. Lamper)

6.30 p.m. — Presentation of Prizes in Village Hall by Mrs. Youngman

7 p.m. — WHIST DRIVE (18 hands) in the Village Hall

8.30 p.m. to Midnight — DANCE to Laurie Hendy and his Music
The Village Hall, Admission 2/6   All proceeds to the New Kennington Sports Ground

FRIDAY EVENING, SEPT. 25th, at 6.15 p.m.—
COMIC FOOTBALL MATCH in Kennington Meadow

If Wet the Fete will be held in the Village Hall and Men's Club Room

Regal Press, Wilkins Road, Cowley, Oxford

The field was prepared and seeded by Messrs Sutton & Sons of Reading at a cost of £400 and various events, including a fete, were organised to raise this further sum of money.

A proper pavilion was opened on the Playfield sports field on 9 July 1962. The plaques read *'These facilities were provided with the help of a grant from the National Playing Fields Association'* and *'This playing field was given to the Kennington Parish Council for public use by E A Sutton Esq of Coventry 5 acres, F J Wiles? Esq of Oxford 2 acres.'*

'A comic cricket match between Kennington Girls' Venture Club and Kennington Cricket Club was watched by a large crowd on Kennington Meadows last night. The players were in fancy dress and the match ended in a draw. Mr Norman Chasney was umpire and the match was organised by Mrs Margaret Simpson (Girls' Club) and Mr Len Peedell (Cricket Club). At the close the umpire, who had periodically drenched players with buckets of water during the game, was ceremoniously thrown into the river.' Oxford Mail report c1951. Left to right back row: Colin Underwood, –Enock, Len Peedell, –, George Butler. Front row: Dickie Godfrey, Maurice Petts, –, Jack Lamper, Mr Thomson, Jack Lawrence.

The girls team comprised, left to right back row: Audrey Tuffrey, Janet–, Margaret Simpson, Muriel Villebois, Jill Spencer, Esther Goddard, Jackie Howard, Margaret Beyer, Sally Underwood, Ann Picking, Gwyneth Thomas.

Kennington Football Club 1937-38 season. Left to right back row: Albert Allen, Stan Allen, George Moss, Charlie Saywell, Bill Dale, Ron Trinder, Jack Blakeman, Harold Cox. Middle row: G Bloomfield, Maurice Petts, Albert Carr, Les Hewer (Captain), Sid Trinder, Pat Morris, Sid Tuck. In front: Len Peedell, Ron Hewer.

Football team of c1958. Left to right back row: Fred Day, Len Peedell, Roger Hambridge, John Legge, Frank Walters, Arthur Berry. Front row: Norman Chasney, George Butler, —Griffiths, Jimmy Clarkeson, Bryn Giles, Les Wacknell.

The Kennington Kestrels, a cycle speedway team, was formed c1952, on a site where the health centre has now been built. The opening of the track attracted a very large crowd. The vicar, the Rev John Dixon is on the left with George Simpson, chairman of the parish council, on the right.

The Kestrels team, left to right back row: Brian Kemp, 'Basin' Smith, —, —, Colin Underwood. Front row: Pat Lamper, Alan —, Barry Jackson, Ray Ledger. The cycle track was eventually moved to a site behind 181 Poplar Grove.

Celebrating a win for the Kennington Kestrels, left to right back row: Jack Kerby, —, Mr Jack Lamper. Front row: Mr Smith, Audrey Kerby, Hazel Kerby, Flo Kerby, Mrs Smith, Mrs Lamper. Mr Lamper's son rode in the Kestrels, and Mr Lamper was one of the organisers.

An impressive display of medals for the Kennington Kestrels. Left to right: Pat Lamper, —, 'Basin' Smith, —, 'Babe' Ledger, Barry Jackson, —.

An Aunt Sally team from the Scholar Gypsy c1960. Left to right back row: Billy Fullick, Bob Butler, John Davis, —. Front row: Avril Fullick, — Richard Wallington, Les Gardner landlord, Tommy Tait, Jack Godfrey. The Scholar Gypsy had been built in 1957.

Kennington Boys Football Club c1975. Left to right back row: Mark Donkin, Chris Griffin, Andrew Pitter, Les Wacknell, Paul Phillips, Craig Joyce, Ian Bolton, Paul Crooks, Gary Brain. Front row: Alan Clapton, Kevin James, Dick Archer, John Hitchin, Ian Pitts, David Fifield, Ian Walters.

Kennington Boys Football Club c1975. Left to right back row: Simon Cook, Mark Tinson, Steven Mail, Kevin Horseman, David Wacknell, Carl Walters, Raymond Sturgess, Peter Holland. Front row: Graham Underwood, Will Gardner, Paul Brown, Paul Gordon, Paul Barrett? —.

Kennington Boys Managers Team 1983, at the annual Boxing Day match against the boys. Left to right back row: Don White, Geoff Dighton, Alan Jefferies, Brian Evans, Stuart Hickman. Front row: Bert Scott, George Ross, Dennis Fogden, Peter Biggs, —. It would seem that the team were sponsored by the Scholar Gypsy.

Kellys Directory 1937. (Reed Information Systems)

KENNINGTON is a small village, and was formed into an ecclesiastical parish February 16th, 1866, out of the parishes of Radley and Sunningwell; it is separated from Oxfordshire by the river Isis and is on the high road from Oxford to Abingdon, 2 miles south from the former, 4 north from Abingdon and 2 miles north from Radley station on the Birmingham and Oxford branch of the Great Western railway, in the Abingdon parliamentary division of Berkshire, hundred of Hormer, petty sessional division, rural district, county court district and rural deanery of Abingdon, archdeaconry of Berkshire and diocese of Oxford; the Thame branch of the Great Western railway passes through the parish and the branch crosses the river here over a bridge of three arches. The church of St. Swithun, built and consecrated in 1828, is a small edifice of stone in the Norman style, consisting of nave and a western bell-cote containing one bell. There are 80 sittings. In the garden of the manor house are some remains of the earlier church. The parishes of Kennington and Radley were reunited in August, 1904. The register dates from the year 1829. A burial ground of over an acre in extent was given for the use of the parish by Edgar Norton Disney esq. and consecrated by the Bishop of Oxford in August, 1914. The living is a vicarage, gross yearly value £354, in the gift of the Bishop of Oxford, and held since 1918 by the Rev. Charles Abdy Marcon M.A. of Oriel College, Oxford, who resides in Oxford. The soil is principally stone brash, resting on the limestone. The crops are grain in succession. The area is 430 acres; the population in 1931 was 738.

SUB-POST & TELEPHONE CALL OFFICE.— Walter . Stenning, sub-postmaster. Letters arrive through Oxford, which is the nearest M. O. & T. office

National School, Miss Drew, mistress; Miss James and Miss Glue, assistant mistresses

County Police station

PRIVATE RESIDENTS.

Acaster Rd. Verona
Acott Mrs. Strathmore
Adams Brian, Rosedene, Radley rd
Adkins-Harry J. New Orleans
Allen Albert E., Septembre. Telephone No. Boars Hill 177
Allen Mrs. Allendale
Allen Norman, Kinfauns, Radley rd
Allen Thos. Woodbine ho
Allen Tom, Willow bank, Bagley wood
Anderson Rt. H., Chessington
Argyle Gilbt. J. Brunbale
Arkell Thos., St. Lawrence, Upper rd
Arkell Wm. Hy. Sunset view, Upper rd
Avery Arth. Scriplea villas
Barber Wm. Chas. Croft cott
Barbour Miss J. N., Lawn
Baskerville Alfd. Thos., Glendalough, Radley rd
Bawden Aubrey E. Lynford, Radley rd
Beesley Harold M. Ann Arbor, Radley rd
Bennett Jas. Hazeldene
Benwell Wm. A. Lido
Berry Chas. Edwd. Gwynfa, Upper rd
Billing Hy. Avoca, Upper rd
Blakeman Leslie R., Strathmore
Blofeld Loris, Copgrove cott
Bloomfield Graham Fredk., Te Rangi
Boore Alfd., Ferndale, Upper rd
Bowden Jn. Cornwood
Bowden Percyl. Peverell, Radley rd
Brookes Thos. W. Yokohama
Broomfield Fredk. Graycote, Bagley wood
Brown Vernon, Cartref
Brundle Lennox, Earlswood
Burgess Fredk. Wm. Thorncliffe
Burton Archbld. Riverview
Butler Chas. Marion Lea
Butler Wm. Geo., Eastbury
Canning Regnld. W., Bram cote
Capel Barry, The Warren, Radley rd
Carter Jn. F. The Firs, Upper rd
Chamberlain Wm. Geo. Uplands, Radley rd
Chapman Cyril, Lyndale
Chilton Jn. Wm. Dardoni, Radley rd
Clutsom Tom B., Quantock
Cook Albt. Wm. Tregantle, Radley rd
Cooper Geo. Osmond, Lane cott. Bagley wood
Copp Mrs. W. J. Manor ho
Cornell Jn. Buncaster
Cox Frank, The Cofrey
Cox Geo., Ridgeway
Cox Harold, Hill crest
Craigmuir Jn., Péronne
Cross Misses, Woodlands
Cummings Albt. Redroots, Upper rd
Currie Donald L., Cranthorpe
Davies Regnld., Windrush
Davies Wltr. Edwd. Whitecliff
Day Sydney Wm. Jn., Belmont
Dowse Michael. Marigold
Draper Alfred, Lynton
Draper Horace, Cranwell
Drew Jack T., The Maples, Sandford la
Durbridge Clifford Jack J., Curnock head, Upper rd
Ellis Ross, Springfield cott
Elston Alfd. St. Veep cott
Eustace Albt. Knowle
Farrer Mrs. Copgrove
Faulkner Fras. W., Harmer, Bagley wood
Faulkner Jn. Arcadia, Upper rd
Fensome Stanley A., Riversbend, Radley rd
Field Chas., Stanlea, Radley rd
Field Miss, Ilsley
Fore Mrs. Teneriffe, Upper rd

Francis Frank Geo. Glenroy, Upper rd
Furby Ernest Fredk. W. Haventhorpe
Furley Percy Arnold, Pinewood
Gandy Edwd. R. Green close, Upper rd
Gibbons R. J. The Dairy
Gibbons Thomas, Lowlands
Gifford-Ambler Christphr. The Bungalow
Gobey Mrs., De-Eli, Radley rd
Goddard Stanley Alfd., Bagley gro
Godfrey Jas. 1 Upper rd
Godfrey Mrs., Jasmine cott
Granger Geo. Jn., Maybury
Gray Wm. G. Downside, Upper rd
Green Alan Montague, Honily, Upper rd
Green Edwd., Woodrow, Upper rd
Green Ivor Fredk. Suvla Bay, Radley rd
Hackett Saml. C. Hillcrest, Radley rd
Harris Hector G., St. Aubins
Hartwell Horace, The Bungalow, Bagley wood
Hatred Saml., Upway
Hebborn Hy. 2 Alexandra villas
Hemmings Raymond, 2 Upper rd
Hewer Fredk. Dalwood
Hobby Geo. Arth. Nettleham
Honey Jas., Cherwell
Horne Mrs. Nestledown, Upper rd
Horrell Mrs. The Quinces, Upper rd
Howard Frank, White lodge
Howard Rt., Glenlea, Upper rd
Howkins Horace V. Sandfield, Sandford la
Hughes Geo. Grasmere
Hughes Geo. Alfd., Homeleigh, Upper rd
Humphries Gerald B. Geraldene, Radley rd
Hunt Jn., Wood View, Radley rd
Jackman Sidney, Castlecroft
Jackson Regnld. Montlhery
James Edwin Oliver, The Nook
Jones Frank, St. Swithuns
Jones Jas. Stanley, Ellenglade
Kerry Rd., Woodthorpe
Kimber Harry, Thames view
King Chas., Kendal
King Jsph. Lawrence, Fairfield, Radley rd
King Percival Henry, The Hawthorns
Kirk Geo. Arth. Bagley-Frith
Knight Gilbt., Phyll-Mar, Upper rd
Knight Sydney, Springfields, Upper rd
Lawrence Frank, Chalelm, Radley rd
Lee Percyl. D. Fir Tree bungalow, Upper rd
Lewis Albt. Leonard
Lightwood Ralph, The Homestead
Livesey Alan A., St. Clare
Lloyd Jn. Edwin, Mounthill
Longthorp Wm. Viney, The Stone ho
Lord Cyril J. E. The Rise, Sandford la

Luckett Mrs. M. L., Chalêt, Upper rd
McPherson Jn. S. Elderslie
March Fredk. Jn. 3 Alexandra villas
Margerison Louis Caleb, The Cottage, Bagley wood
Massey Rt. R
Matthews Fredk. E., Burville, Upper rd
Mattingley Fras. D., Ingledene
Maydon Wm. Hy. Hartleydene, Upper rd
Merry Geo. The Lawsons
Miers Miss J. N. Edenhurst
Mills Percy Stuart, Dunromin
Morris Mrs. Restholme
Mullins Percyl. The Mount, Upper rd
Mundy Miss, Woodside
Musgrove Thos. Hy. Greengrove, Upper rd
Nobes Harold, Bagliffe, Upper rd
Palmer Mrs. Ada, Perthur
Pearce Fredk. Cyril, Kinetonville
Peedell Geo. Belinda cott
Peedell Jn. A. Bryher
Perry Fras. Jn., Southcot, Sandford la
Petts Maurice, Aymestrey, Sandford la
Pitts Geo. Danl. Chilson ho
Poole Geo. Jas., Knutsford, Radley rd
Pope Gilbt., Pfalz
Pye Jack, Suntona
Pye Miss Holly, Bermuda
Raworth Chas. S. Cranbrook ho. Radley rd
Roberts Ernest L. The Elms
Robinson Montague, Lyndhurst
Rockall Miss, Polurrian
Rowles Geo. Hy. Steepholm
Rowles Herbt. S. Lyssenhoek
Saunders Maurice Edward, Beaconsfield
Saywell Chas. Edwd., Cheswyn
Scarrott Archbld. Lucerne
Scarrott Chas. L. Lorna-Doone
Shaw Howard Fras. Dawn bungalow
Sherwin Alfd., Ayredale, Upper rd
Sibbald Jas. Bydand
Simkins Frederick William, The Hollies
Simpson Geo. Keen, Maundown
Sims Sidney, Budleigh, Upper rd
Smallbone Bernard, Gibraltar house
Smewin Geo. E., Clanley
Smewin Wm. Jas. Tralee
Smith Albert William, Underwood
Smith Ernest H., Dalmeny
Snelling Gordon Wm., Kenmore
Sopote Mrs., Onar, Upper rd
Spracklen Charles, Brockenhurst
Stroud Harry Jas., Rosslare
Sutton Sydney Jn., Whitehaven
Taylor Ralph, Valmaur
Theobald Chas. Wm. Cumberford

Townsend Percyl. Devonia, Radley
Trevelyan Rev. Jn. C. St. Veep
Trewin Ernest Geo., Maywood, Upp
Tuck Sidney, Sandown
Tuffrey Peter, Melbourne ho
Tuffrey Wm. Leonard, Clovelly
Turner Wltr. Brookside Upper rd
Underwood Albt. Treverlyn
Underwood Hy. Jn., Undershaw, Upp
Viner Edwd. Eden, Upper rd
Walker Horace Wm., Sherwood, Upp
Walklett Fras. Jn., Cranleigh, Uppe
Walters Albt., Windyridge
Walters Jsph. Calgary
Wastie Stanley A. L. New ho
Way Harry Jn., Chez-nous
Webb Jn. Hazelton
Weeks Mrs. E. Lamorna
Westell Cr s. Nags view, Sandford
Westell Harry, The Corner, Radley
Weston Fredk. Wm. Alvaston
White Mrs., Swinford, Sandford la
Wichall Fredk. Glengarry
Williams Rd. Maison Stanley
Williamson Rev. Wilfred Alex. Southwood
Williamson Thos., Tudor ho
Willis Lawrence A. Iverna, Radley r
Wisby Jas. Albt. Haslemere, Radley
Wood Harry, Derry Vale
Wrigglesworth Norman, Athlone, Upp
Wright Jn. Wm. Ringwood; Upper
Wright Wm., Lichfield
Wyatt Albt. Percy, Orchard lea
Wyatt Ernest H., Sandbanks, Upper
Wyatt Mrs. Sylvia Dean

COMMERCIAL.

Allen Albert E. builder, Septem Telephone No. Boars Hill 177
Barson Arthur John, newsagent, stationer, tobacconist
Berry Victor, insur. agt. Gwynfa, Uppe
Chasney Horace, Tandem P.H
Cosendey Chas. tea gardens, Merwede
Cowley Haulage & Coal Co. haulage tractors (order office), Septembre
East Wm. dairyman
Faulkner F. W. laundry, Bagley wood
Finch B. V. plumber
Howse Leonard, greengro. The Rosar
Imperial Forestry Institute (rese nursery)
Jeffery Leonard Stanley, insur. Greenways, Upper rd

Kennington and its People

Floods in 1947. The Red Bridge is to the right of centre, with Kennington on the left hand side.

'The entrance to Kennington, along Kennington Lane from the Red Bridge, was constantly under flood water. It was suggested that the road should be raised, but as a compromise we put a wooden flood path along the sides. This was fine for a year or so, but lorries were constantly going in and out of the pits, and they needed to have access. The wooden path was therefore made to be moveable, on wheels, but following a really good flood these were easily destroyed, and you would then need to jump 12 to 18 feet to get across - or walk round the long way.'

During bad flooding buses used to go up the Old Abingdon Road through Sugworth and then down through Little London. In 1947 water was up to the window cills at the first bungalow coming into Kennington.

Flooding on 31 December 1979 and flood water halts traffic at the northern end of the main Oxford to Kennington road, near the entrance to Templeton College, formerly the Oxford Management Centre.

'Between Upper Road and the Red Bridge were two gravel pits and a large rubbish dump. Over the years the pits filled with water, and were used for skating during the winter months. Right in the middle there used to be an old bus, raised up on barrels out of the floods. The sweep and his sons lived there and they used to chase us off the dump. If you wanted your chimney swept he had a small letter box and you used to slip a note in. Beyond that there were wooden sheds that had belonged to the gravel pits and I believe some people lived there.

Along by the Management Centre there used to be coloured gypsy wagons, the proper traditional sort. They used to make their pegs out of willow trees, put together with a bit of tin round them held with a tac, and sell pegs and flowers at Christmas — those queer wooden flowers they used to whittle out of wood. During the war there was a camp along by the college — on the piece of land all planted now with horse chestnut trees. One of the gipsies bought that strip of land and there was almost a permanent encampment there.

Upper Road used to be called Green Lane and the approach, the 'First Turn' from Oxford, was a rough cart track in the 1930s, smothered in brambles and brushwood, with four or five great big elms on the corner and a stream running down the side. There was a rough piece of field, known as Kitty's Field, where Mrs Avery kept the pony she used with her trap to get into Oxford to her drapers shop. The moon daisies used to grow almost waist high and there was a small pond in the field where we used to catch tadpoles. This track was covered with boulders and you couldn't ride a bike down there, you had to go down Kenville Road.

My uncle lived at 39 Upper Road, known as Sunset View. Down the garden was an old wooden summer house, with a fireplace and a chimney, made of weather boarding with an earthen floor. The people who had the plot before had used it as a weekend retreat. Many people bought quite large plots of land, very cheap some of them, and built a shack, almost a holiday home. Years later these plots of land sold for thousands.'

Number 37 Upper Road, called St Lawrence after the Canadian river, seen here in 1931. Left to right: Annie Arkell, Mrs Maud –, Thomas Charles Arkell. Children: Kathleen Arkell, Janet Arkell, Jessie Arkell, with boy cousin. '*Upper Road was an unmade road, just grass and an absolute morass in winter. We weren't on main sewer or water and when the well ran out we had to carry water up from the spring down by the signal box, beyond Stone House.* There were pumps and wells all over Kennington and '*in a drought we had in the '30s the water was like ditch water and we couldn't drink it.*'

Bill Gray had the University School of Forestry where Forest Side is now. This photograph was taken on the day the Forestry closed, in the early 1970s, and includes Brenda Noble, Jean Godfrey, Ivy Wyatt, Ivy Berry, Connie Lanham, Hilda Morris, Gladys Cox, Mrs Pitts, Cic Peedell, Gladys Wyatt, Mr Tom Brooks, Harold Doman head woodman, Cyril Atkins, Bill Gray.

The Francis family lived at No 41 Upper Road, known as Glenroy, a bungalow which was demolished about 1994/5 for the development of Old Nursery View. Frank and Margaret Francis moved to Kennington in 1928. This photograph shows Margaret Francis in front of Glenroy in May 1937.

The Francis family in 1946, back row left to right: Sylvia Tomlyn née Francis, Jack Francis, Les Ball, Edgar Francis, Ray Francis. Middle row: Doris Francis with Margaret, Margaret Francis, Frank Francis, Alice Ball née Francis with Alan. In front: Cyril Ball, Peter Ball, Sylvia Francis, Joyce Ball, Sonia and Helen Francis.

The Lawns in 1999. The land originally belonged to the Disney family, but was conveyed in 1908 possibly for the construction of the property. The original terms of the conveyance of 1908 stated *'the purchaser shall erect sufficient cattle proof and sheep proof fences not less than 3 feet 9 inches nor more than 5 feet high along the north east, north west and south west sides of the land.'* Only one house was allowed costing not less than £500. The Lawns Estate, as it was known, was purchased by Percy Jarvis who erected the original house. Mr Jarvis also purchased adjoining land with permission for a further house, or a pair of houses,

again costing no less than £500, but he did not carry out this further development. During the 1920s and 30s the house belonged to Mr Jack Archer Pye, of Pye builders. Mr Jack Pye obtained Mr Edgar Norton Disney's agreement to vary the terms of the original contract, for the cost of ten shillings. *'I remember the Lawns as a dairy farm with cows going up and down across Upper Road twice a day. There was a short cut from Upper Road to Kennington Road past the Lawns, with cow sheds on the left of the house.'*

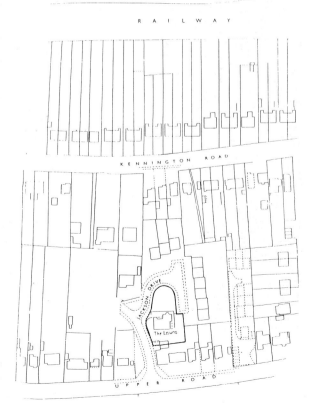

The Lawns was originally approached via a long drive from Kennington Road, but now stands in Jackson Drive, named after Reg Jackson a parish councillor.

At the far end of Upper Road, near the roundabout and the alley to Little London, stood a little tin hut where Mr and Mrs Eric Thompson lived. They are seen here in a photograph c1910. Mr Thompson was a verger in St Swithun's church. The building was an old army hut bought and erected by Mr Thompson. It was known as Rolleston Hut, apparently named after an area on Salisbury Plain. In June 1923 local newspapers reported 'The Kennington Sensation', when Edward Frederick Radbone, aged 31, and Emma Louisa, his wife, and Miss Harriet New were charged with the manslaughter of his son, aged 18 months, at Rollestone Hut.

KENNINGTON LANE

A postcard dated 1929, from the bottom of Edward Road towards Oxford. The road was always known as Kennington Lane. The white picket fence on the right hand side still exists amongst the thick hedging. Many of the early properties were called 'the old temporaries'.

One such 'temporary' building was 135 Kennington Road, known as 'Cumberford', seen here in 1930. The building was originally timber framed, but was later given a concreted outer layer. The home of Charles and Edith Theobald for many years, seen here with Sylvia. When this was demolished in 1998 it was regarded as *'one of the last temporaries'.*

Charles and Edith Theobald as they are best remembered in the village.

'Cumberford', 135 Kennington Road, at the time of VJ celebrations in 1945, with Edith and Sylvia Theobald.

Miss Beatrice Webb and William Pitter of Park Farm Radley on their wedding day at Kennington church in 1923. Mr and Mrs Pitter lived at 137 Kennington Road.

Charlie Kerby, a local builder, seen below c1957 outside 81 The Avenue. Note the sign C F Kerby & Son, outside the property. Mr Kerby built many of the council houses in modern Kennington, including the original council housing in Poplar Grove. He was a special constable for 30 years, and was often to be seen in his uniform. He died on 20 February 1997, the day before his 93rd birthday.

'The first properties I built in Kennington were twelve bungalows in Poplar Grove. I also built those four houses opposite the co-op, down that dip. I bought the ground. It was three old cottages there that were burnt down and they were sort of patched up afterwards and people lived in them for some years and after they got condemned I bought them off the people that owned them. We used a lot of the stone and wood from the cottages to level the ground as best we could. There used to be two little gateways up on the road, at the side of the footpath, and you went down long paths to the three cottages.'

Kennington Road c1939. The property on the left, now the co-op stores, had previously been Dunstons, the village post office. Wiggins took over in 1938 and the premises became a general store; the post office, under Mr Faulkner, moved to the corner of Edward Road, to premises that had previously been Lewis's, a greengrocer and *'a bit of a taxi service'*. Mr Lewis is remembered as having only one eye. Faulkner *'had an encyclopaedic memory and could remember every parcel you posted over the previous five years.'* This small building can be seen here on the left on the corner of Edward Road, with the small wooden Memorial Hall on the right.

The post office on the corner of Edward Road which was demolished c1961 when owned by Derek Ledger.

Opposite the post office was Ava Cottage, number 165 Kennington Road, home to the Shayler family. Mrs C O Shayler, Mrs Jackson, Mr Arthur J Shayler and Gerald Shayler on the Bicester Road, Oxford c1941.

Arthur Shayler died on 21 December 1950. He had run a shoe repair business from about 1914, for much of that time from 165 Kennington Road, opposite Edward Road and next to the Memorial Hall. The business closed in 1956 when the property was sold. Mr Shayler had a petrol engine with a dynamo in a shed out the back of the shoe repair shop. This provided electric light for the house and ran the machinery. This was in great demand from the Memorial Hall and they paid for petrol to run the dynamo for a dance or similar event. Number 165 Kennington Road, Ava Cottage, and number 167, Bryhar Cottage are still standing. Number 161 Kennington Road was Lowlands, occupied by Mr and Mrs Gibbons, where Mr and Mrs Shayler took lodgings immediately after the First World War.

Mr Arthur Shayler was the village shoe and boot repair business. The old boot shop is on the right in the above picture, with the late Mrs Vera Shayler.

This cottage, one of three, used to stand on the Kennington Road, next to the old church and in front of the present-day site. This photograph c1930 shows Mrs Selina Godfrey. Her husband Jack Godfrey, often refered to as 'Man' Godfrey, was a farm worker for the Manor Farm.

A very old photograph of Jack Godfrey driving the farm cart. It is not known where this was taken, but is believed to be in Kennington. When Mr Godfrey died in the 1990s a memorial stone was erected to him in Bagley Wood.

The same cottages were damaged by fire shortly before they were demolished c1950.

Outside the cottages in Kennington Road, opposite the church, in front of Dr Blackman's present house, c1904. Arthur, John and Flo Webb.

The Avenue in 1947, with the distinctive 'Dip' which was often flooded (R H G Simpson). The Avenue had formerly been just a footpath, the Radley Footpath, from Cow Lane, behind the old church and across the fields to Radley. This footpath was well used by the Radley clergy during the time when Kennington was in that parish. Following Sir George Bowyer's acquisition of land in Kennington, and his mining activities within the district, he formed The Avenue for his convenience, as the most direct route from Kennington to his home in Radley, now Radley College. Development along the Avenue started c1938.

Sydney Harris came to 'Upways' in Little London c1932, which he rented while his property in Sugworth Lane was being built. Outside 'Upways' in the mid 1930s, left is Reg Winter with Sydney Harris on the right. At this time the majority of properties in Kennington depended on paraffin for both cooking and lighting. Mr Harris started a paraffin round, delivering with a horse and cart before progressing to a motorbike delivery round. During the war business was continued by his wife, Mrs Elsie Harris, at which time deliveries were done from a van.

Bagley Wood has been woodland for at least 1300 years. There is mention of Bagganwurthe, the homestead or street of Baggan, possibly a lost chapelry in the locality of Bagley Wood, in a charter of 956. In 1557 St Johns College acquired a portion of the Wood, and subsequently all of it. By 1850 Bagley Wood had been enclosed, and the people of Hinksey and Kennington were no longer allowed to gather wood.

Little London, or Bagley Wood Road as it is now, was just a collection of cottages, most of which were occupied by men who worked in nearby Bagley Wood, employed by St John's College. They were always a separate community and had their own well which was situated at the beginning of St Swithun's Road.

'Mr Pitter's parents came and lived in a cottage there. Little Mrs Siddens was a well known character. St Swithuns Road had not been built, and down at the bottom which now would be right in the junction of the road was a communal well with a bucket and handle for water for Little London. Mrs Simms lived in a wonderful little cottage, one up and one down. She used to stand at the gate 'like little Mrs Tiggywinkle in the Beatrice Potter book'.

Sydney Harris outside the Grandpont Bakery which was owned by George Back who was also a fellow angler, in the early 1950s. Bake's bakery operated a regular delivery round throughout the village.

Local boys in the fields in Kennington pre-war. Left to right back row: Peter Chilton, Ivor Horn, Ron Bowden, John Cummings. Front row: Ron Harris, Tony Taylor.

Sarah and Walter Trinder with George c1929 at Spinney Piece. Walter was chauffeur and gardener for Bagley Wood House next door.

W H East Dairy Farmer of Kennington in the late 1920s. Left to right Mrs Hannah East (Maurice's grandmother), Mrs Geraldine Petts (Maurice's mother), and Maurice Petts outside 21 Little London, 'the Big House' next to the dairy, where Granny East lived. Maurice Petts moved from his family home in Bletchley to Kennington in 1922, at the age of 10, to help his uncle, Bill East, with the dairy in Little London. Part of this little farm had been used as a football field, prior to the founding of the Playfield Grounds.

Granny Hannah East in front of 'the Big House', 21 Little London. *'It was a funny place. One side of it had tiles at the side, there was a cellar with three rooms down and three bedrooms.'*

Bill East with his wife Doris and young Gillian, seen here c1934. Bill East inherited the dairy from his mother, Hannah East. The dairy was then run by Maurice Petts until he retired from the business in 1955.

Maurice Petts in Little London, with the dairy farm buildings in the background. *'there never used to be a playing field as such, but the Kennington boys used to play football up Little London. On the left hand side next to the dairy there used to be a field, a cow field, and on Saturdays we used to put goal posts up and that used to be Kennington football field. It was on a slope and of course there were a lot of cow pats about. If you kicked the ball too hard it would go into the pit - that's still there, roughly opposite the Scholar Gypsy at the bottom of those gardens. We used to play in this pit when we were children.'*

Number 13 Sandford Lane, built c1934 by Maurice and Ruby Petts.

Maurice and Ruby Petts on their golden wedding anniversary, 29 August 1984, at 13 Sandford Lane. Ruby was in service in Bagley Wood Road where Maurice met her while doing his milk round. Later she worked at the local co-op and during the war had helped her husband with the dairy rounds.

Children gathered in the Village Hall for the 1953 Coronation celebrations.

Kennington Road looking north towards Oxford. Wych-Elm Cottage is on the right and the Tandem in the far distance.